M000273463

HEALTHY LIVING JAMES

HEALTHY LIVING
James

JAMES WYTHE

Photography by Clare Winfield

CONTENTS

INTRODUCTION

Ever since falling ill, and throughout
my ongoing recovery, I have been keen
to identify and help others suffering
from similar health issues, as well as
promoting a healthier lifestyle to those
wanting to improve their well-being.
My passion is to create recipes to make
living healthily easy, tasty and fun
for everyone.

MY STORY

The last 11 years have been quite the journey for me. On 4th December 2010, I went out for a meal with friends feeling completely fine, but when I woke up the following morning, I could barely move. I felt extremely nauseous, dizzy and could not get out of bed. Little did I know that my whole life was about to change.

Growing up I had always been an extremely active, happy and sporty guy. As a child, I regularly competed in swimming galas and played for my school's football, rugby and hockey teams. Aged 10, I took up golf and soon realised that this was the sport for me. By 13, I was in the Dorset junior team and, aged 15, I was one of the youngest-ever members of the Dorset men's first team. I travelled around the country competing in national tournaments, and I knew that golf was the career path for me. I then went on to study sports coaching and development, initially at Merrist Wood College and then at Bournemouth University, where I gained a BSc Sport and Exercise Science degree and represented their first team at golf.

Then things drastically changed. It all started just a couple of months after completing my degree at Bournemouth. I thought my illness after that night out was just a touch of food poisoning, but for some reason I didn't recover and the symptoms just seemed to get worse and worse. I tried to push through this but reached a point where my dad had to physically carry me into the doctor's surgery. I remember the doctor talking to me and the only word I could reply with was 'ambulance'. I was immediately rushed into hospital for a suspected brain tumour. I had several brain scans, which all came back fine. I had lost nearly 3 stone in weight and couldn't talk, eat, drink or even stand up!

I was kept in for 11 days and tested for everything they could think of, however all the tests came back 'normal'. At that point, I had also become hypersensitive to more and more of the medication they were giving me. One of the medicines gave me an anaphylactic reaction, which left me struggling to breathe and was incredibly scary. I also developed a sensitivity to light, smells and certain foods. The doctors were unable to give any diagnosis apart from saying that I had some kind of viral infection, so they just sent me home and told me to rest and take it easy for a while.

I did go home and rest, but unfortunately I didn't recover or feel any better. In fact, I just got worse. I was bed-bound, unable to stand up or walk by myself. I couldn't watch TV or look at my phone as I was extremely sensitive to the light, which would give me awful headaches. And to make matters worse, I suffered from severe insomnia, often going days without any sleep at all.

After multiple attempts to get help from the doctors, it was nearly 6 months before they finally diagnosed me with ME (Myalgic Encephalomyelitis), also known as CFS (Chronic Fatigue Syndrome). I was told there was no 'cure' and all I could do was rest and wait. It was a bittersweet feeling as I finally had an answer, but I was also being told there wasn't any cure, which left me feeling very worried.

My mum refused to accept that my life going forward would be like this and put all her time and energy into finding answers. She arranged for a nutritionist to visit me and it was then that I was advised to cut out gluten and dairy from my diet, which I did immediately. Having made these first adjustments to the way I ate, over the next 12 months I slowly began to see improvements in my health. I was at last able to get out of bed and walk to the window (a mere 2 metres away) and I could finally hold a conversation that lasted longer than 5 minutes. For me, these were huge achievements. During the 2 long years of being confined to my bed, the one thing that kept me going was telling myself that I would get better and that as soon as I did, I would help inspire others in similar health situations. I could not accept that this was it for me, and I knew that someday I would get to share my story to support and motivate other people.

During my bed-bound stage, I withdrew myself from all social situations and had to back away from most of my friends, many of whom questioned the truth of my condition. The last thing I needed was to be judged or told to just get out of bed. It was easier to be alone. Then a girl called Luise miraculously came into my life. We had met through mutual friends before I was ill, but we had hardly spoken. She heard I wasn't well and asked if she could come and visit me. I came up with endless excuses as to why it wasn't a good idea, but she kept insisting. I was incredibly nervous but ended up saying yes and I am so grateful I did. Luise would turn up day after day, even though it was a 90-minute round trip, and just sit on the end of my bed and talk to me.

She said she knew I would get better and that she wanted to be part of this journey with me. We fell in love and have been through this whole 11-year adventure together, from her seeing me at my worst, having to carry me to the toilet, to watching me take my first steps, and then me being able to see her walk down the aisle at our wedding in 2018. She has been an incredibly important person in my life and helped so much with my recovery. Luise was there from the start and is now chief recipe tester for the blog!

After 2 years of being confined to my bed, and then recovering at a very slow pace, Luise and I decided to move into a flat together in Bournemouth. Luise was still at Bournemouth University and also working part-time to pay our rent, so I was home alone more often than not and had to again push myself outside of my comfort zone in order to feed and take care of myself.

Top left: This was my first walk outside after 12 months of being bed-bound. It felt like the world had gotten a lot bigger once I stepped out.

Top right: Luise and I met whilst I was at my worst and she never failed to turn up, no matter what. She was always there, even if it was just to sit by my side.

Bottom right: We decided to take a big step and move in together. This was scary as I was still bed-bound at this stage, but my food journey was just beginning.

Bottom left: Our wedding day. This felt like such a milestone in our journey together – one of the best days of my life!

During that time, I taught myself how to cook from scratch with the precious 5 or 10 minutes of energy I had. I took a chair into the kitchen so that I could sit down and rest whilst making my food. I soon discovered that I really liked researching and preparing healthy, fresh food, as well as looking for quick gluten- and dairy-free dishes as I didn't have the energy to cook for hours.

My passion for food began to grow, and I saw the incredible results it was having on my health and mental well-being. Cooking became my daily challenge. It was what got me out of bed three times a day. During the 10–15 minutes that I was cooking, I completely forgot what I couldn't do anymore and focused entirely on what I was now able to achieve.

During 2015, my friends and family began to show an interest in my passion for cooking and encouraged me to share my healthy and easy-to-make recipes with them. So, I decided to start a blog. I was nervous about this first step, but I thought it would be a brilliant way of storing recipes for my own use and for easily sharing with close family and friends. I had no idea that, a few years later, you would have this recipe book on your shelf!

At the start of 2016, I began to build my website, typing up and photographing my recipes, and by August 2016, *Healthy Living James* was born.

Eleven years into my recovery journey, *Healthy Living James* continues to be an incredibly rewarding and inspiring project for me. I am at a stage where I can now look back and see what a huge impact food has had on my recovery. And I keep discovering more ways to eat healthily, without making it super complicated or time consuming.

Ever since falling ill, and throughout my ongoing recovery, I have been keen to identify and help others suffering from similar health issues, as well as promoting a healthier lifestyle to those wanting to improve their well-being. My passion is to create recipes to make living healthily easy, tasty and fun for everyone. That includes those suffering from long-term illness, people with allergies and intolerances, vegans and vegetarians alike.

I have been totally amazed by the support of my readership over the last 5 years. The daily messages from followers who have suffered from, and continue to suffer from, the incapacitating effects of illness really move me. Although my recovery is by no means over and I have my bad days, it gives me great pride to have inspired others through my journey, along with sharing my ups and downs in an honest and relatable way. Many of my followers have been looking forward to the day I publish a recipe book. It's been my biggest dream, which has finally come true, so I really hope you will dive in and cook as many recipes as possible!

COOKING & MENTAL HEALTH

During my health struggles, cooking became my daily challenge. It was what helped me out of bed three times a day and gave me a task to focus on. During the small window of time that I was cooking, I didn't think about all the things that had drastically changed in my life and instead thought only about the recipe I was making. It was like I was in my own little safe bubble and I forgot about everything else that was happening around me.

In those days I was very anxious, constantly worrying about how I was going to get back to health. All these thoughts went on inside my head:

'Can I ever have a normal life?'

'Will I be able to play golf again?'

'I want to be well enough to travel and see more of the world – is that going to happen?'

'Is a long walk or a bike ride something I won't be able to do in my future?'

'Will my friends understand this new me?'

Cooking became an outlet for me to stop those thoughts. When I was in the kitchen, it was like nothing else mattered. My entire focus was on making a recipe taste great. I saw it as a mental challenge to use the supermarket ingredients I had delivered to the house and turn them into a healthy dish using the least time or effort possible.

The thing that helped me to enjoy cooking was changing my mindset and trying to see cooking as a hobby rather than a chore. I started to enjoy the preparation of chopping, tasting the food along the way, and the best part was seeing the smile on someone's face when they tucked in.

I find cooking a way of expressing myself and helping me to connect with others. For me, it's a way of bringing the people that matter to me the most together for a chat and to enjoy each other's company.

The satisfaction I feel when making a recipe from scratch is incredibly rewarding, especially when I share it with family and friends. It's something that you achieved and can feel proud of, no matter how big or small. You made it!

Even now, being mostly recovered and creating recipes as my 'job', I still find cooking is my safe place and something that gives me purpose. It can be an

incredibly powerful tool to help with mental health. It has helped me more than I can even write in this book, and I know it can help so many others out there too.

So, go on and follow some of the recipes in this book. I promise it will help take your mind off everything else that is going on and the end product will be something you'll be proud of. You don't even have to tell your partner and/ or friends that it wasn't your recipe, it will be our little secret!

ABOUT THE BOOK

This is the book that I really needed when I was housebound and struggling with my health. I had no idea how to cook and very little energy to concentrate on complicated instructions. What I wanted was a simple cookery book with quick and easy, healthy recipes, short ingredients lists and basic instructions. I couldn't find any suitable books, so I decided to teach myself how to cook from scratch.

I wanted to create this recipe book with accessibility in mind. My aim is to encourage those who are short on time, new to cooking, lacking in confidence or struggling with their health into the kitchen to have a go at making delicious dishes at home using affordable supermarket ingredients.

Life can be very fast-paced and it's all too easy to rely on takeaways and convenience foods. Shopping for food, preparing and cooking takes time but with health and well-being becoming increasingly important for many of us, I feel my recipes can really help. The recipes are all suitable for those suffering with food allergies or ill health and I guarantee you won't be spending hours in the kitchen.

ABOUT THE RECIPES

I have created over 80 easy, delicious and inspiring recipes using affordable supermarket ingredients that I hope will become your new favourites.

The recipes are all:

Gluten-free: I use gluten-free flours and naturally gluten-free ingredients. However, I also offer options to swap in gluten-containing ingredients if you're not gluten-free.

Dairy-free: I cook with alternative plant-based milks and cheese or make my own creams and sauces, but again, I do offer options for those who still can, or want, to consume dairy.

Egg-free: I'll show you how you can bake healthy desserts without the need for eggs.

Refined-sugar-free: I use maple syrup, honey or coconut sugar in all my recipes as I feel they work and taste the best in these types of desserts.

Mainly plant-based: There are a couple of amazing fish recipes in this book, but I do feel we all need to eat more plants for health and environmental reasons. This book is about helping you discover easy, affordable, veg-packed meals so you don't feel like you're missing out.

Simple to follow: Being dyslexic, I have always struggled to read instructions, especially when they're long-winded. I break down each recipe with a step-by-step approach to cooking from scratch, with colour photographs for every recipe to help you visualise the food, along with easy-to-read ingredients lists and instructions.

FAQs on each recipe: I try to answer the most common questions you might have about each recipe to enhance your cooking experience.

Suitable for vegetarians, vegans & flexitarians: I offer options within the recipes to help cater for all.

NOTES ON INGREDIENTS

Due to the fact that I have multiple food allergies and so have made certain food choices, I have used ingredients in this book that suit my lifestyle. However, I want to make my recipes accessible to all, so I have written them in a way that means you can choose which of these ingredients you prefer to use to suit your lifestyle and food choices. Below are my notes to explain what ingredients will work best for you:

Flour: I am gluten intolerant, so I use gluten-free versions of all the flours listed in this book, but you can use gluten-containing equivalents if you wish. I haven't found there to be much difference in cooking times/results.

Milk: I have a dairy allergy, so I have to follow a strictly dairy-free diet. My favourite alternative milk that I have used throughout this book is unsweetened almond milk. However, there are so many good choices now, such as coconut milk, oat milk, soya milk, etc. You can use whichever milk you prefer throughout the book.

Cheese: As I have a dairy allergy, I have used vegan cheese alternatives throughout this book, but you can simply swap for dairy-containing cheeses if you wish with the same results.

Butter: I have cooked with vegan butter throughout this book and I stick to a firm block of butter rather than the spreadable margarine as I find it works better in the dessert recipes. You can of course simply swap for dairy-containing butter.

Yoghurt: I have used unsweetened coconut yoghurt in the recipes, but again, you can swap for soya or even plain dairy/Greek yoghurt if you prefer.

Meat-free: I decided to stop eating meat about 2 years ago, so all the recipes in this book are meat-free, though some contain fish. I have used sausages in some recipes where I choose to use vegan ones, but again you can use whichever suits your lifestyle. I have also mentioned in some recipes that you can adjust to add meat or fish if you wish.

Sugar: I use refined-sugar-free ingredients in my recipes due to finding that these have helped my blood sugar levels throughout my recovery. I opt for granulated coconut sugar but you can swap for brown sugar if you wish. I also use maple syrup as a liquid sweetener as I love the flavour it adds, but you can swap for runny honey if you're not vegan.

Baking powder: NOT all baking powder is gluten-free, so if you are coeliac or have a gluten intolerance, then always read the packaging.

Cacao powder: I cook with cacao powder as it is made from fermented beans that haven't been roasted, whereas cocoa is processed at a much higher temperature and is often mixed with other ingredients, such as dairy or sugar. Having said that, you can use whichever you prefer in my recipes as they will work very similarly.

Coconut milk: I use full-fat versions over light. Yes, they contain more calories, but they create a much creamier texture and taste much better in curries and desserts.

Dried herbs & spices: An absolutely essential part of my kitchen, dried herbs and spices are affordable, last for ages, and pack dishes full of flavour. Check out my shopping list on page 23 to see which ones I recommend.

Garlic granules or powder: These are a must-have on your spice/herb shelf. They are affordable and help to add flavour quickly into dishes without the need for fresh ingredients.

Gram flour: Often used in Indian cuisine and also known as besan flour, gluten-free gram flour is made from chickpeas and can be bought in most supermarkets in the world foods section.

Hemp, flax & chia seeds: These are brilliant ingredients that can add extra protein and nutrients into smoothies.

Miso paste: A brilliant ingredient that I use a couple of times in this book. You can get it in most supermarkets now in different variations. I personally prefer brown rice miso paste for its dark colour but you can use standard or white miso to the same effect.

Nutritional yeast: A great way of adding a quick 'cheesy' flavour to sauces if you're vegan or dairy intolerant. It can be found in most supermarkets in the free-from or vegan aisles.

Oats: These are naturally gluten-free but if you suffer with coeliac disease or are gluten intolerant, it's advisable to opt for special gluten-free oats as standard oats are often cross-contaminated during processing methods with wheat, barley or rye. You can find porridge or rolled oats in most supermarkets, but either will work in my recipes so use whichever you have/prefer.

Oil: When frying at a low temperature I often opt for olive oil. When frying at a high temperature, I swap for coconut oil due to its higher smoke point. I also find coconut oil adds an extra layer of flavour in certain recipes, such as curries and some desserts. When deep-frying, I use a basic vegetable or rapeseed oil.

Pasta: I often opt for brown rice pasta as it's naturally gluten-free and I think it tastes the best. However, you can use whichever pasta you want in the recipes.

Protein powder: An optional extra for the kitchen cupboard, which can be used in smoothies or shake-and-take oats to boost the protein content. I opt for a vegan vanilla protein powder but any whey protein will work too.

Quinoa: Naturally gluten-free, quinoa is actually a seed and not a grain. It's easy to prepare and can be found in most supermarkets now. It is much safer to store and reheat than rice, so you can make big batches of it.

Rice: Makes a great gluten-free side dish and I serve it with all the curries in this book. I often opt for brown rice due to its higher nutrient content, but when in a rush I will also use white rice as it takes half the time to boil.

Self-raising flour: I use a pre-made blend of gluten-free self-raising flour. This is available in most supermarkets, but if you only have plain flour, just add 3 tablespoons of baking powder and 1 teaspoon of xanthan gum per 500g of plain flour to help it rise a little more.

Tamari: A gluten-free alternative to soy sauce, which can be found in most supermarket free-from aisles.

Tinned beans: I use pre-cooked tinned chickpeas, black beans, butter beans and cannellini beans very often and they are a staple ingredient in my store cupboard. You can prepare your own beans from the raw form, but I personally find this adds a lot of time for not enough gain.

Tinned lentils: Similar to tinned beans, I opt for using pre-cooked tinned lentils over preparing my own due to speed in recipes.

Vegetable stock: I prefer to use veg stock powder, which is available in most supermarkets, but you can also use veg stock cubes or pots. 1 teaspoon of veg stock powder equates to 250ml (1 cup) liquid, so you can adjust this to the cubes/pots if you use those instead. Also, not all vegetable stocks are gluten-free, so just be aware if you are coeliac or gluten intolerant and check the labels.

SHOPPING LIST

Here is a list of the core cupboard ingredients that I always try to have in my kitchen. It's a great starter kit for those wanting to try more of my recipes. If you have the majority of these ingredients, you'll be able to make most of the recipes in this book without the need to shop for more apart from the odd fresh ingredient. I order the bulk of these online to be delivered to help reduce time and save energy on carrying it all.

All of the ingredients listed are either used multiple times in the recipes or have a long shelf life, so you won't buy and end up wasting them.

Along with the cupboard ingredients opposite, I always try to have a few fresh ingredients to hand such as garlic, red onions, lemons and limes as I use these quite often in my recipes.

TINS
Chickpeas
Full-fat coconut milk*
Chopped tomatoes
Beans (black, cannellini, kidney
   & butter beans)*
Green lentils*
Sweetcorn

JARS
Tamari (or soy sauce if you can
   tolerate gluten)*
Passata
Mustard (wholegrain & Dijon)
Peanut butter
Cider vinegar
Miso paste*
Oil (coconut, olive & sunflower)*

FLOUR
Plain*
Self-raising*
Buckwheat
Gram*

FROZEN
Frozen peas
Frozen spinach
Berries (blueberries & blackberries)

BAGS
Oats (rolled or porridge)*
Red split lentils
Quinoa*
Rice (risotto & brown basmati)*
Pasta*
Rice noodles

DRIED HERBS & SPICES
Ground coriander
Cayenne pepper
Paprika
Smoked paprika
Chilli flakes
Ground turmeric
Ground cinnamon
Basil
Oregano
Thyme
Sage
Dill
Rosemary
Bay leaves
Garlic granules or powder*
Fennel seeds
Sesame seeds

BAKING
Baking powder (check it's
   gluten-free)*
Maple syrup (or runny honey)*
Coconut sugar (or brown sugar
   if preferred)*
Cacao powder*

NUTS & SEEDS
Cashews
Pine nuts
Walnuts
Ground almonds
Hemp, flax & chia seeds*

OTHER
Veg stock powder, cubes or pots*
Tomato purée
Nutritional yeast*

*Check the Notes on Ingredients on
  pages 18–20 for more information.

BREAKFAST & BRUNCH

BANANA WAFFLES

SWEET POTATO & BEAN HASH

EVERYDAY BLUEBERRY SMOOTHIE

CHOCOLATE PEANUT BUTTER
SHAKE & TAKE OATS

EASY BLUEBERRY OAT MUFFINS

THE BEST FLUFFY PANCAKES

NO-BAKE 15-MINUTE GRANOLA

STRAWBERRY GRANOLA POT

SWEET OR SAVOURY CRÊPES

Breakfast is the least creative meal of the day for most, so I want to give you some inspiration with healthy but still quick and easy ways to start the day. From my go-to weekday breakfasts for one to weekend breakfasts to share, this chapter has everything covered.

BANANA WAFFLES

Super-easy, five-ingredient waffles. Whip up a plate for breakfast, brunch or dessert – they're good at any time of day!

Makes 2
Prep 5 mins
Cook 10 mins

150g rolled or porridge oats
1 large banana
2 tbsp maple syrup or runny
  honey
2 tsp ground cinnamon
250ml (1 cup) milk of choice

1. Add all the ingredients to a blender and blend until a smooth batter forms.

2. Allow the mixture to sit for a couple of minutes to thicken whilst your waffle machine heats up.

3. Pour half the mixture into your waffle machine and cook with the lid off for a couple of minutes before placing the lid down onto the waffle. Cook until the waffle machine bleeps (roughly 5 minutes). Repeat with the second waffle.

4. Serve with your favourite toppings.

FAQ

What toppings do you suggest?
Try a simple berry sauce, made with a generous handful of mixed berries and 1 tablespoon of sweetener (maple syrup or honey), added to a pan and simmered down until soft.

Can't eat bananas? Swap the banana for 60g (½ cup) apple sauce.

Which oats are best for this? I tested it with both rolled and porridge oats and they work the same.

Don't have a waffle machine?
Try making as pancakes instead. Just allow 10 minutes for the batter to thicken before pouring into a lightly greased pan to fry.

SWEET POTATO & BEAN HASH

One of my favourite recipes for a healthy start to the day, this hash is packed with lots of colourful veg and flavour.

Serves 2
Prep 10 mins
Cook 20 mins

1 small sweet potato
½ red onion
1 garlic clove
1 red pepper
4 mushrooms
1 tin (400g) black beans
oil, for frying
1 tsp paprika
1 tsp ground coriander
pinch of chilli flakes
2 handfuls of kale or spinach
juice of 1 lime
1 avocado (optional)

1. Firstly, slice the sweet potato into very small cubes and cook in salted boiling water for 5–7 minutes until they just start to soften.

2. Meanwhile, dice the red onion, crush the garlic clove and roughly chop the pepper and mushrooms. Drain and rinse the black beans.

3. Once the sweet potato is partially cooked, drain and set aside.

4. Now, add a glug of oil to a large frying pan along with the onion, garlic, black beans, pepper, mushrooms, spices, sweet potato cubes and some salt and pepper, then fry together for 7–8 minutes.

5. Finally, add in the kale or spinach and lime juice. Stir together and fry for a further 2 minutes until the kale or spinach has softened.

6. Top with the sliced avocado (if using) and serve straight to the table.

FAQ

Can I swap for other beans? Absolutely – try cannellini or butter beans instead. You could even use chickpeas.

Don't like sweet potato? Use white potatoes instead.

EVERYDAY BLUEBERRY SMOOTHIE

This is my go-to morning smoothie. I have this three or four times a week as it's so easy and fills me up until lunch.

Serves 1
Prep 3 mins

125g (1 cup) frozen blueberries
1 ripe banana
2 tbsp cacao powder
2 tbsp ground flaxseed
1 tbsp hemp seeds or chia seeds
250ml (1 cup) milk of choice

1. Simply add all the ingredients into a blender and blend until smooth.

FAQ

Can I use other berries? You could use mixed berries if you prefer.

Can I add in extra protein? Sure, add a small scoop of protein powder if you wish.

ALL-DAY BREAKFAST TRAYBAKE

An easy, healthier version of a recipe I have missed since becoming gluten- and meat-free.

Serves 3–4
Prep 10 mins
Cook 50 mins

500g potatoes
1 garlic clove
1 tsp dried basil
1 tbsp oil
4 large tomatoes
150g mushrooms
2–3 large spoonfuls of
  Homemade Smoky Beans
  (page 50) (optional)
6 sausages of choice
  (I use meat-free)
4 frozen spinach blocks

1. Preheat the oven to 220°C/200°C fan/gas 7.

2. Now, chop the potatoes into small cubes.

3. Add them to a roasting tray, top with the crushed garlic and the basil, pour over the oil and season with salt and pepper. Mix until well combined, then roast for 25 minutes.

4. Meanwhile, slice the tomatoes and mushrooms in half and prepare the beans, if using.

5. Remove the potatoes from the oven and add the tomatoes, mushrooms, sausages, beans and the spinach blocks.

6. Mix and bake again for 20–25 minutes until browned.

FAQ

Can I use tinned beans instead? Sure, swap the smoky beans for ½ × 400g tin of baked beans.

Can I use fresh spinach instead? It will burn if you bake it, so wilt it separately in a pan, then mix through after the traybake has been cooked.

CHOCOLATE PEANUT BUTTER SHAKE & TAKE OATS

One of my favourite filling breakfasts – perfect for an on-the-go morning when you need something more than just a smoothie.

Serves 1
Prep 5 mins
Stand 10 mins

60g rolled or porridge oats
1 tbsp cacao powder
1 tbsp maple syrup or runny honey
1 tsp peanut butter (crunchy or smooth)
185ml (¾ cup) milk of choice

1. Add all the ingredients in the order listed opposite to a jar, place the lid on and shake.

2. Leave to sit for 10 minutes and it's ready to eat.

FAQ

Want to turn it into overnight oats? Simply use 250ml (1 cup) milk instead of ¾ cup and place in the fridge overnight.

Peanut allergy? Try other nut butters, such as almond.

Nut allergy? Simple leave out the peanut butter or add 1 tablespoon of chia seeds instead.

Can you add toppings? Absolutely – I love topping mine with coconut flakes, cacao nibs or berries.

EASY BLUEBERRY OAT MUFFINS

These are such a tasty on-the-go breakfast or snack. They're filling, packed with bursting blueberries and incredibly easy to make!

Makes 6
Prep 10 mins
Cook 15 mins
Cool 15 mins

3 small ripe bananas
160g (2 cups) rolled oats
2 tsp ground cinnamon
1 tsp baking powder
60g blueberries
60ml (¼ cup) milk of choice
oil, for greasing

1. Preheat the oven to 200°C/180°C fan/gas 6.

2. Peel and mash the bananas in a large bowl.

3. Add all the other ingredients and mix together until well combined.

4. Lightly grease a muffin tin with oil or line with paper.

5. Spoon in the mixture to the top of the cups (it should fill 6).

6. Bake for 12–15 minutes.

7. Remove from the oven, carefully take out the muffins and place on a cooling rack for 15 minutes.

FAQ

Can I use porridge oats instead?
Yes, they will work, but the muffins won't quite have the same texture and will be denser.

What can I swap the bananas for?
Try apple sauce instead, roughly 125g (1 cup).

Can I use other berries instead?
Absolutely – try raspberries or blackberries.

Mine are still too wet in the middle?
If you have made sure to leave them to cool for 15 minutes and they are still a little soft inside, then bake for 5 minutes longer next time you make them.

THE BEST FLUFFY PANCAKES

Light, airy and delicious without needing gluten, dairy or eggs!
This is the most popular pancake recipe I have ever made and
they will become your new go-to pancakes!

Makes 6
Prep 5 mins
Cook 15 mins
Stand 5 mins

200g self-raising flour
   (I use gluten-free)
1 tsp baking powder
2 tsp chia seeds
1 tbsp melted coconut oil, plus
   extra for frying
3 tbsp maple syrup or runny
   honey
250ml (1 cup) milk of choice

1. Add all the ingredients in the order listed opposite to a
   large bowl and whisk until smooth. Allow to sit for 5 minutes
   to thicken.

2. Heat 1 teaspoon of coconut oil in a large pan on a medium
   heat until it melts.

3. Pour in a sixth of the mixture from a height (this helps to
   keep the pancakes round) to make your first pancake.

4. Fry the pancake for about 1 minute on each side, until lightly
   golden, then make the rest of the pancakes.

5. Serve with maple syrup or your favourite toppings.

FAQ

Don't have self-raising flour? Use plain
and add 1 more teaspoon of baking
powder (2 teaspoons total).

Don't have chia seeds? Swap for ground
flaxseed or leave them out – the
pancakes will still work.

Can you use other oils? Sure, swap for
sunflower oil.

How do I know when to flip them?
Wait until you see little bubbles appear
on the top.

NO-BAKE 15-MINUTE GRANOLA

An incredibly easy, one-pan granola that doesn't even need you to turn on the oven. Once you try this, you won't go back to baking it!

Makes 6–8 servings
Prep 5 mins
Cook 10 mins
Cool 10 mins

3 tbsp coconut oil
6 tbsp maple syrup or runny honey
240g (3 cups) rolled oats
1 tbsp ground cinnamon

1. To a large non-stick pan, over a low/medium heat, add the coconut oil and maple syrup or honey and stir until the coconut oil has melted.

2. Now, add the oats and cinnamon and stir until well combined.

3. Fry for roughly 5 minutes, making sure to stir every minute.

4. Take off the heat and allow to cool for roughly 7–10 minutes.

FAQ

How can I make it into clusters? Once you take it off the heat, press down all the oats firmly with a spatula until they form a base and allow to cool. Once cooled, gently break them up and they will form clusters.

How long will it last? For a few weeks in a sealed jar at room temperature.

Can I use another oil? Yes, other oils should work just as well.

Can I add extras into it? Sure, try adding in seeds, nuts or coconut flakes when adding the oats.

STRAWBERRY GRANOLA POT

A healthy spring/summer breakfast that you can prepare the night before for a quick grab-and-go breakfast in the morning.

Serves 1
Prep 5 mins

100g strawberries
150g coconut yoghurt
4–5 spoonfuls of No-Bake
   15-Minute Granola (page 42)

1. Firstly, add the strawberries to a blender and blend into a liquid sauce.

2. Now, in a large bowl, layer up the yoghurt, strawberry sauce and granola as you wish.

3. Either serve straight away or store in the fridge overnight.

FAQ

Can I use other berries? Try it with any berries you wish or even a mixture.

Can I add extras? Sure, try adding nuts or seeds for extra protein.

SWEET OR SAVOURY CRÊPES

A naturally gluten-free buckwheat crêpe that can be enjoyed
with sweet or savoury ingredients depending on what you fancy!

Makes 4
Prep 5 mins
Cook 10 mins

125g (1 cup) buckwheat flour
375ml (1½ cups) cold water
oil, for frying

Sweet topping ideas
coconut yoghurt
blueberries
maple syrup or runny honey
lemon juice

Savoury topping ideas
mushrooms
spinach
sliced cherry tomatoes
fresh herbs
sliced avocado

1. Add the buckwheat flour and cold water to a large bowl and whisk until smooth, then allow to sit for a few minutes.

2. Meanwhile, heat a crêpe pan (see FAQ if you don't own one) with a small drop of oil.

3. Pour in a thin layer of the batter and tilt until the whole pan is evenly covered.

4. Fry on each side for 1–2 minutes, making sure to be careful when flipping. Repeat with the remaining batter to make 4 crêpes in total.

5. Now, prepare your sweet or savoury toppings based on what you fancy.

FAQ

How would you serve the savoury toppings? I personally would chop the mushrooms and fry in a little oil for a few minutes, then add in the spinach and herbs and fry together until the spinach wilts. Pile onto the crêpes with sliced avocado and wrap up.

How would you serve the sweet toppings? I would simply pour them over the top or wrap them up inside.

I don't have a crêpe pan? Use a medium non-stick frying pan instead.

TASTY TOFU SCRAMBLE

A tasty tofu alternative for those that can't eat eggs!

Serves 2
Prep 10 mins
Cook 10 mins

400g firm tofu block
1 tbsp oil
2 tbsp nutritional yeast
2 tbsp milk of choice
1 tbsp wholegrain mustard
1 tsp ground turmeric
¼ tsp garlic granules or powder
toast (I use gluten-free)

1. Firstly, drain and press the tofu as per the packet instructions. Personally, I wrap it up in kitchen paper and place a chopping board on top to press out the excess liquid.

2. Heat a pan with the oil and crumble the tofu directly into the pan.

3. Add the other ingredients with a generous pinch of salt and pepper. Mix it all together and fry for 7–8 minutes.

4. Serve with toast.

FAQ

What is nutritional yeast? See page 19 for more information.

Is nutritional yeast essential? No, you could leave it out if you wish.

HOMEMADE SMOKY BEANS

Easy homemade beans you can make in under 15 minutes using mainly cupboard ingredients.

Serves 4
Prep 5 mins
Cook 10 mins

oil, for frying
2 garlic cloves
2 × 400g tins haricot or cannellini
   beans
1 tbsp smoked paprika
350g passata or 1 tin (400g)
   tomatoes
2 tbsp tomato purée
125ml (½ cup) water
1 tsp veg stock powder
   (or ½ stock cube)
1 tbsp maple syrup or runny
   honey
toast (I use gluten-free)

1. Add a glug of oil to a large pot on a medium heat and crush the garlic directly into the pot to fry for a minute.

2. Now, add the drained beans, smoked paprika, passata, tomato purée, water, veg stock, maple syrup or honey and some salt and pepper.

3. Stir and simmer for 8–10 minutes until it reaches the desired consistency.

4. Serve with toast.

FAQ

Can I freeze leftovers? Yes, just allow to cool first.

What do the beans go with? Try adding them to the All-Day Breakfast Traybake on page 34.

LUNCH ON THE GO

COURGETTE & BROCCOLI FRITTERS

BAKED FALAFELS

GRILLED PRESSED WRAP

SHAKE & TAKE BEAN SALAD

SMASHED CHICKPEA SANDWICH

SWEET POTATO & LENTIL SALAD

TEX-MEX QUINOA SALAD

HOMEMADE POT NOODLE

SAUSAGE ROLLS

Finding lunch whilst out and about when you have food allergies is nearly impossible, so I always create my own to make sure I have something to eat. This chapter is packed full of my favourite healthy lunch recipes, which will give you energy throughout the day.

COURGETTE & BROCCOLI FRITTERS

A great way of using up that leftover courgette and broccoli in the fridge, add the fritters to salads for the perfect lunch on the go.

Makes 4
Prep 5 mins
Cook 10 mins

1 courgette
½ head of broccoli
juice of 1 lime
handful of chopped fresh
    coriander or parsley
1 tsp paprika
1 tsp ground coriander
70g (½ cup) gram flour
125ml (½ cup) water
oil, for frying

1. Grate the courgette into a large bowl.

2. Finely chop your broccoli into small pieces, so you have about the same amount as the courgette.

3. Add to the bowl with the lime juice, herbs, spices, flour, some salt and pepper and the water and mix together.

4. Heat a large frying pan with a couple of tablespoons of oil.

5. Shape the mixture into 4 large fritters, adding a bit more flour if it is too wet to hold together, and place in the pan.

6. Fry for roughly 5 minutes on each side until golden brown.

FAQ

What is gram flour? See page 19 for more information.

Can I use another flour? Yes, try using a plain flour instead.

Can I bake them instead? Sure, place onto a baking tray lined with baking paper and bake for 20–25 minutes at 200°C/180°C fan/gas 6.

BAKED FALAFELS

Easy-to-make falafels that are baked instead of fried to make them healthier. I love adding them into wraps or using them to top salads.

Makes 12
Prep 10 mins
Cook 25 mins
Cool 15 mins

1 red onion
4 garlic cloves
1 tin (400g) chickpeas
oil, for frying
1 tbsp ground coriander
1 tbsp smoked paprika
pinch of chilli flakes
handful of fresh coriander
    leaves and stalks
handful of fresh parsley
    leaves and stalks
60ml (¼ cup) olive oil
35g (¼ cup) plain flour
    (I use gluten-free)

1. Preheat the oven to 220°C/200°C fan/gas 7.

2. Roughly dice the onion, crush the garlic and drain the chickpeas.

3. Pour some oil into a large pan over a medium heat and add these, along with the dried spices, and fry together for 5 minutes.

4. Now, spoon this all into a food processor, along with the coriander, parsley, olive oil, flour and a large pinch of salt and pepper. Pulse into a paste (you may need to push down the edges with a spatula and pulse again).

5. Shape into roughly 12 small patties and place onto a baking tray lined with baking paper.

6. Bake for 20 minutes.

7. Allow to cool for 10–15 minutes as this helps them to firm up.

FAQ

Can I fry these instead? Sure, bring a pan with oil to a high heat and fry the falafels until crispy.

How shall I serve them? Perfect for topping salads or try them with the Red Onion Hummus (page 182) or in the Grilled Pressed Wrap (page 60).

GRILLED PRESSED WRAP

My take on the social media sensation!

Serves 1
Prep 5 mins
Cook 5 mins

1 large wrap of choice
    (I use gluten-free)
3 falafels
2 tbsp hummus
small handful of grated cheese
    of choice (I use vegan)
small handful of salad leaves

1. Firstly, make a cut from the centre of the wrap to its edge, then imagine the wrap as 4 quarters.

2. Add the falafels to one of the quarters, the hummus to another and the cheese to the opposite half (see page 62).

3. Gently fold over the sections along the cut to form a triangular pizza slice shape with the fillings stacked on top of each other.

4. Heat a griddle pan and fry on each side for 2–3 minutes.

5. Slot the salad leaves into the natural pocket the wrap forms and eat straight away.

FAQ

Which falafels shall I use? Try my Baked Falafels recipe (page 58).

Which salad is best? I love it with rocket for its peppery taste.

Which hummus should I use? Try my homemade Red Onion Hummus (page 182).

SHAKE & TAKE BEAN SALAD

A protein-packed salad that you can batch prep for 3 days.
Add all the ingredients to a lunchbox, shake and take on the go.

Makes enough for 3 lunchboxes
Prep 15 mins

1 tin (400g) black beans
1 tin (400g) green lentils
1 fennel bulb
3 celery stalks
8cm piece of cucumber
handful of baby plum tomatoes
1 mango
handful of fresh parsley
3 tsp cider vinegar
3 tsp maple syrup or runny honey
3 tsp olive oil

1. Drain and rinse the beans and lentils together in a colander.

2. Roughly chop the veg, tomatoes, mango and parsley.

3. Prep 3 small rectangular containers, adding the chopped ingredients along with an even amount of beans and lentils.

4. Top each container with 1 tsp of the cider vinegar, maple syrup or honey and olive oil. Season with salt and pepper.

5. Place the lid on the containers and shake.

6. Store in the fridge for up to 3 days.

FAQ

Can I use a different vinegar?
Yes, any should work.

Can I mix up the veg? Absolutely, this is just giving you some guidance. By all means use any veg you have.

SMASHED CHICKPEA SANDWICH

This is one of my favourite sandwich fillers. It will have you hooked from the first time you try it.

Serves 4
Prep 5 mins

1 tin (400g) chickpeas
2 heaped tbsp coconut yoghurt
juice of ½ lemon
1 tbsp olive oil
handful of fresh parsley or dill
sliced ciabatta, baguette or wrap
   (I use gluten-free)

Extras
salad leaves
sliced tomato

1. Firstly, drain the chickpeas and add to a large bowl.

2. Roughly mash with a potato masher or fork.

3. Now, add the yoghurt, lemon juice, olive oil, chopped herbs and a pinch of salt and pepper and mix until well combined.

4. Simply serve in a sandwich with your favourite extras.

FAQ

How long will this last? The filler will last about 3–4 days in a sealed container in the fridge.

Can I make it oil free? Sure, simply leave out the oil if you prefer.

Which yoghurt do you recommend? I have tested it with both unsweetened coconut and soya yoghurts.

Can I use it to top anything else? Absolutely, try topping a baked potato with this mix – it's delicious!

SWEET POTATO & LENTIL SALAD

A healthy, veg-packed, super-filling recipe that can be batch-prepared on the weekend for delicious packed lunches.

Makes 3 lunches
Prep 10 mins
Cook 25 mins

1 sweet potato
2 large carrots
1 red onion
3 tbsp olive oil
1 tin (400g) green lentils
2 handfuls of rocket
2 handfuls of watercress
½ block (100g) feta or cheese
    of choice (I use vegan)
1 tbsp maple syrup or runny
    honey
1 tbsp cider vinegar

1. Preheat the oven to 200°C/180°C fan/gas 6.

2. Chop the sweet potato and carrots into small cubes and slice the red onion into quarters. Place onto a baking tray with 2 tablespoons of the olive oil and a pinch of salt and mix together.

3. Bake for 25 minutes.

4. Meanwhile, add the lentils, rocket, watercress, chopped feta, remaining olive oil, maple syrup or honey and cider vinegar to a large bowl and mix.

5. Once the veg are roasted and golden, allow to cool, then stir into the salad and season with salt and pepper.

6. The salad is now ready to serve up or place into lunchboxes for another day.

FAQ

How long will the salad last if meal prepping? Place into containers, allow the veg to cool and store in the fridge for up to 4 days.

What can I swap for the lentils? Try using any tinned beans, such as black or butter beans.

TEX-MEX QUINOA SALAD

This is probably one of my favourite meal prep lunches. It can be made on a Sunday evening for the whole week ahead.

Serves 5
Prep 10 mins
Cook 20 mins
Cool 20 mins

200g (1 cup) quinoa
250ml (1 cup) veg stock
250ml (1 cup) water
1 tin (400g) black beans
1 tin (200g) sweetcorn
1 red pepper
1 avocado
handful of fresh coriander
juice of 1 lime
½ tsp paprika
¼ tsp chilli flakes
¼ tsp garlic granules or powder
2 tbsp olive oil

1. Firstly, add the quinoa to a small sieve and rinse with cold water until the water runs clear, then add to a pan.

2. Now, add the stock and water to the pan, place the lid on and simmer for 15–18 minutes.

3. Meanwhile, prepare the other ingredients by draining the black beans and sweetcorn and adding to a large bowl. Chop the pepper and avocado into cubes and roughly chop the fresh coriander. Add all these to the bowl with the lime juice and mix.

4. Now, add in the spices, garlic granules and olive oil and mix again.

5. Once the quinoa is cooked, drain the excess water (if any) and allow to cool for 15–20 minutes before adding to the bowl and mixing it through.

FAQ

How long will it last? For up to 5 days in a sealed lunch container in the fridge.

Is there a faster way to prep this? Sure, use precooked packed quinoa instead of cooking your own if you're in a rush.

HOMEMADE POT NOODLE

A healthy, homemade take on the pot noodle. Simply add all the ingredients to a jar, then all you will need is boiling water and a fork.

Serves 1
Prep 10 mins
Stand 10 mins

½ red pepper
3–4cm piece of fresh ginger
1 small carrot
30g rice noodles
70g (½ cup) peas
small handful of fresh coriander
    or parsley
¼ tsp garlic granules or powder
juice of 1 lime
1 tbsp tamari
1 tsp miso paste
375ml (1½ cups) boiling water

1. Firstly, prep the vegetables by chopping the pepper into small cubes, finely dicing the ginger and peeling long strips of the carrot with a peeler. Gently crush the rice noodles to make smaller.

2. To a large jar, such as a Kilner jar, add the peas, pepper, carrot, herbs, ginger, garlic granules, lime juice, tamari, miso paste and rice noodles and press all of them down into the jar.

3. When ready to eat, just add the boiling water, place the lid on and shake. Leave to stand for 7–10 minutes to allow the noodles to soften.

FAQ

Not gluten-free? You could swap the tamari for soy sauce.

How far in advance can you prep this? I would say 2 days before with all the veg. Store in the fridge and just add the boiling water when ready to eat.

Can I use frozen peas? Yes. If making this recipe to eat straight away, then make sure to add the peas to boiling water first to allow them to thaw out, otherwise it reduces the temperature of the pot noodle too quickly and won't cook the noodles.

SAUSAGE ROLLS

Super-simple sausage rolls you can make with whatever sausages you want. One of my favourite recipes in this book.

Makes 12–14 small rolls
Prep 10 mins
Cook 20 mins

1 gluten-free puff pastry sheet
6 sausages of choice (I use
    meat-free)
1 tsp dried sage (optional)
2 tsp Dijon mustard
olive oil
sesame seeds (optional)

1. Preheat the oven to 220°C/200°C fan/gas 7.

2. Unroll the pastry sheet and slice down the middle so you have 2 long sheets. Place on a baking tray lined with baking paper.

3. Squeeze out the sausage meat from the skins into a bowl, add the sage and mash with a fork.

4. Add the sausage mix to the middle of each pastry sheet and shape into a sausage to fill.

5. Now, gently brush the top of the sausage mix with the mustard.

6. Fold the pastry over the sausage, brush the edges with water and seal all the way round by pressing down with a damp fork.

7. Cut 3 slits across the top of each sausage roll, brush with olive oil and add a sprinkle of sesame seeds.

8. Bake for 20 minutes until golden and crispy.

FAQ

Can I prepare these in advance?
Sure, just leave to cool and then store at room temperature for up to 24 hours. You can store in the fridge, but the pastry will lose its crunch.

Can I use another herb rather than sage?
Absolutely, try basil or oregano.

WEEKLY STAPLES

20-MINUTE FISH CURRY

CREAMY FISH PIE

EASY SHEPHERD'S PIE

MUSHROOM & LENTIL WELLINGTON

MUSHROOM STROGANOFF

SIMPLE SALMON BURGERS

STICKY SESAME STIR-FRY

MISO-GLAZED SALMON KEBABS

THE BEST GLUTEN-FREE PIZZA

This is a chapter of my favourite recipes, which all make it into my weekly rotation. Here I'll show you great tips and tricks to speed up some of your best-loved dishes and how you can pack them with even more veg! If you're ever sat wondering what to make for dinner, this chapter will sort you out.

20-MINUTE FISH CURRY

One of my favourite recipes in this book! It's mildly spiced, incredibly easy to prepare and packed full of flavour.

Serves 4
Prep 5 mins
Cook 20 mins

1 red onion
3 garlic cloves
thumb-size piece of fresh ginger
1 red chilli
oil, for frying
1 tbsp paprika
1 tbsp ground coriander
1 tsp ground turmeric
½ tsp cayenne pepper
250g salmon
250g cod
1 tin (400g) chopped tomatoes
1 tin (400ml) full-fat coconut milk
150g prawns
zest of ½ lime
juice of 1 lime

1. Firstly, dice the red onion and garlic. Peel and chop the ginger and dice the red chilli (remove the seeds if you prefer less spice).

2. Pour a glug of oil into a large pan set over a medium heat, then add the onion, garlic, ginger, chilli and spices and fry together for 5 minutes.

3. Meanwhile, prepare the fish by removing the skin and chopping into decent-size cubes.

4. Add the tinned tomatoes and coconut milk to the pan and bring to the boil.

5. Finally, add the fish and prawns along with the lime zest and juice and a pinch of salt and pepper. Gently simmer for 8–10 minutes.

FAQ

Can you make it vegan? Sure, simply swap the fish for 400g tofu and add a tin (400g) of drained chickpeas.

Can I freeze leftovers? Yes, just allow it to cool before freezing. If using prawns, make sure that they are fresh as you can't cook them twice.

Can I swap for other fish? Absolutely. You could swap for all cod or all salmon, for example. Just try to stick to similar weights.

Is it spicy? I make all my curries on the milder side, so by all means up the spice levels if you wish!

ONE-POT PASTA BAKE

This is the only way I make a pasta bake now as I just love reducing the time and washing-up!

Serves 4
Prep 10 mins
Cook 35 mins

500g pasta (I use gluten-free)
1 tin (400g) black beans
1 tin (400g) cannellini beans
1 tin (200g) sweetcorn
1 head of broccoli or cauliflower
¼ tsp garlic granules or powder
   (or 1 chopped garlic clove)
1 tbsp dried basil
1 tbsp dried oregano
1 tbsp dried sage
1 jar (690g) passata
200g grated cheese of choice
   (I use vegan)

1. Preheat the oven to 220°C/200°C fan/gas 7.

2. Fill a large shallow cast-iron casserole dish or ovenproof pot with water and boil your pasta until al dente.

3. Meanwhile, drain your beans and sweetcorn together in a colander and roughly chop the broccoli into florets.

4. Once the pasta is cooked, drain into the colander with the beans, then add it all back to the cooking dish.

5. Add the garlic granules, dried herbs, passata and broccoli and mix together.

6. Finally, top with the grated cheese and bake for 20–25 minutes until golden and crispy.

FAQ

Can I add meat? Sure, add in chopped chicken with the passata and veg before baking.

What to do with leftovers? Store in the fridge for lunch the next day.

Can I use other beans? Absolutely, just use 2 tins of any beans you want. You could even use chickpeas.

CREAMY FISH PIE

A comforting, dairy-free fish pie that will be the best you've ever made. The white sauce is made using cashews, which are brilliant for creating a creamy sauce.

Serves 4
Prep 15 mins
Cook 45 mins

150g cashews
150g frozen spinach blocks
1 large carrot
200g cheese of choice
   (I use vegan)
1kg white potatoes
250g salmon
250g cod
150g prawns
140g (1 cup) peas
1 tbsp dried dill
juice of ½ lemon
435ml (1¾ cups) milk of choice
1 garlic clove
knob of butter (I use vegan)

1. Preheat the oven to 220°C/200°C fan/gas 7.

2. Place the cashews and frozen spinach in separate bowls, cover with boiling water and leave for 10 minutes. Grate the carrot and cheese. Drain the spinach and squeeze out any excess water with your hands.

3. Now, roughly chop the potatoes into cubes, then cook in a pot of boiling water for about 10 minutes until they soften.

4. Meanwhile, skin and chop your fish and add to a large baking dish along with the prawns, peas, spinach, grated carrot, grated cheese and a generous pinch of salt and pepper.

5. Drain the cashews and add them to a blender with the dill, lemon juice, 250ml (1 cup) of the milk and the garlic and blend into a smooth sauce.

6. Pour the sauce into the baking dish and mix with the fish.

7. Drain the potatoes and add back to the pot along with the knob of butter, remaining 185ml (¾ cup) of milk and a pinch of salt and pepper and mash until smooth.

8. Finally, top the dish with the mash, seal the edges and bake for 30–35 minutes.

FAQ

Can I use different fish? You can use whatever fish you want. You could also just use salmon or cod.

Could I make this with chicken instead of fish? Yes, you could.

Can I make it vegan? You can use 600g of chopped firm tofu instead of the fish or just pack with veggies.

Why don't you peel the potatoes? Not peeling speeds up the cooking time, reduces food waste and increases nutrients, which are in the skins.

Can I use other mash? Yes, try it with sweet potato or parsnip.

Can I freeze it? Sure, but use raw prawns the first time you cook the pie.

EASY SHEPHERD'S PIE

This is the only way I make my Shepherd's Pie! It's as simple as adding the veg to a baking dish, topping with the mash and baking – that's it!

Serves 4
Prep 15 mins
Cook 50 mins

1kg white potatoes
1 small red onion
3 garlic cloves
150g mushrooms
2 carrots
100g (1 cup) walnuts
1 tin (200g) sweetcorn
1 tin (400g) green lentils
140g (1 cup) peas
3 tbsp tamari (optional)
500g passata
1 tbsp dried basil
1 tbsp dried oregano
knob of butter (I use vegan)
185ml (¾ cup) milk of choice

1. Preheat the oven to 220°C/200°C fan/gas 7.

2. Roughly chop the potatoes into cubes and boil for 10 minutes until soft.

3. Meanwhile, dice the red onion, crush the garlic, chop the mushrooms, grate the carrots and crush the walnuts. Drain the sweetcorn and lentils. Add to a large baking dish with the peas, tamari, if using, passata, basil, oregano and a large pinch of salt and pepper and mix.

4. Press the mixture down until it's nice and compact.

5. Drain the potatoes, add the butter, milk and a pinch of salt and pepper and mash until smooth.

6. Top the pie with the mash and then fluff up the potato and seal the edges with a fork.

7. Bake for 40 minutes until golden on top.

FAQ

Can I use any mash? Yes, you can use a different mash such as sweet potato or parsnip.

Why don't you peel the potatoes? A couple of reasons: it speeds up the cooking time, reduces food waste and increases nutrients, which are in the skins.

Not gluten-free? Swap tamari for soy sauce.

Is there a swap for the passata? Sure, swap for 2 × 400g tins of chopped tomatoes.

Can I freeze leftovers? Yes, just allow to cool and then freeze.

MUSHROOM & LENTIL WELLINGTON

This is the perfect main to serve up for a Sunday roast – just add roast potatoes, veg and my Red Onion Gravy (page 180).

Serves 6
Prep 15 mins
Cook 35 mins
Cool 15 mins

1 red onion
2 garlic cloves
1 large carrot
1 large parsnip
1 tbsp oil, plus extra for brushing
1 tsp dried thyme
1 tsp dried rosemary
1 tsp dried sage
2 × 400g tins green lentils
1 tbsp tamari
3 large portobello mushrooms
2 gluten-free puff pastry sheets

1. Firstly, dice the onion, crush the garlic and grate the carrot and parsnip.

2. Now, add the oil to a large pan on a medium heat and fry the onion, garlic, carrot, parsnip, herbs and some salt and pepper together for 5 minutes.

3. Drain the lentils and add to the pan along with the tamari, then stir and cook for a further 2–3 minutes. Take off the heat and allow to cool for 10 minutes.

4. Meanwhile, lay out one of your puff pastry sheets on a large baking tray and preheat the oven to 220°C/200°C fan/gas 7.

5. Add half the lentil mixture to the middle of the pastry sheet, making sure to leave about an inch at the ends and sides.

6. Top with the portobello mushrooms and cover with the remaining lentil mixture, pressing it around the mushrooms until it's compact.

7. Now, you should have a large Wellington shape. Simply top with the other pastry sheet and press it around the mixture. Cut the excess pastry and crimp the edges with a damp fork.

8. Cut 3 slits into the top, glaze with olive oil and bake for 25 minutes.

9. Remove from the oven and allow to cool for 5 minutes before slicing.

FAQ

Not gluten-free? Swap the tamari for soy sauce and use regular puff pastry.

Can I use other mushrooms? If you can't get portobello mushrooms, use 200g smaller mushrooms instead.

What can I serve this with? Serve it with your favourite roast sides, such as roast potatoes, veg and cauliflower cheese and try topping with my Red Onion Gravy on page 180.

MUSHROOM STROGANOFF

This vegan stroganoff has been incredibly popular on the blog, so I just had to include it. Using simple ingredients, it has such a deep and creamy flavour coming from the coconut milk and mustard.

Serves 4
Prep 10 mins
Cook 30 mins

4 garlic cloves
2 red onions
1kg chestnut mushrooms
3 tbsp olive oil
2 tsp paprika
2 × 400ml tins full-fat coconut milk
2 tsp Dijon mustard
juice of 1 lemon
large handful of chopped fresh parsley

1. Firstly, crush the garlic, dice the onion and roughly slice the mushrooms.

2. Heat the oil in a large shallow pan and add the garlic, onion, mushrooms, paprika and a decent pinch of salt and pepper.

3. Cook down for 5 minutes, making sure to stir often.

4. Once the mushrooms have softened, pour in the coconut milk, mustard and lemon juice and stir well.

5. Cook on a high heat (this helps the sauce to thicken) for 20–25 minutes or until the sauce is the desired consistency. Make sure to stir every 5–10 minutes.

6. Finally, add most of the parsley and stir it into the stroganoff, leaving some to garnish before serving.

FAQ

What do you serve this with? I love it with brown rice, on mashed potatoes or mixed into pasta.

Can I freeze leftovers? Absolutely, just allow it to cool and then freeze.

Why won't mine thicken? Use a large shallow pan (this helps to reduce the sauce down faster). If using a pot, it will thicken but just takes longer to reduce.

NO-CHOP BOLOGNESE

This is a great recipe for those that struggle with chopping: simply grab a box grater and grate all the veg, then add to a pan with herbs and a tin of tomatoes for a delicious veggie bolognese.

Serves 4
Prep 5 mins
Cook 25 mins

1 red onion
3 garlic cloves
2 carrots
2 celery stalks
1 tbsp oil
150g mushrooms
100g (1 cup) walnuts
1 tbsp dried basil
1 tbsp dried oregano
1 tin (400g) tomatoes
3 tbsp tomato purée
1 tbsp tamari
1 tin (400g) green lentils
400g pasta (I use gluten-free)

1. Place a large box grater on a chopping board and grate the onion, garlic, carrots and celery.

2. Heat a pan on a medium heat with the oil, add the grated veg and fry for 5 minutes. Pull apart the mushrooms into small pieces and add straight to the pan, along with the walnuts, basil, oregano and a pinch of salt and pepper and fry together for 5 minutes.

3. Now, add the tinned tomatoes, then ½ tin of water (use the tomato tin), the tomato purée, tamari and drained lentils. Stir and simmer on a low heat for 15 minutes.

4. Meanwhile, boil your pasta and drain once cooked.

5. Mix the pasta through the sauce and serve with my Cashew 'Parmesan' on page 190.

FAQ

I don't have a grater? Just finely chop the veg instead.

Can it be nut-free? Yes, simply leave out the walnuts.

Not gluten-free? Swap the tamari for soy sauce.

Can I add beef instead of lentils? Sure, just add the beef to fry in the pan after adding the grated veg.

SIMPLE SALMON BURGERS

I occasionally eat fish and whenever Luise and I crave salmon, these are always top of the list to make! They're super-easy, healthy, have just a handful of ingredients and taste amazing.

Makes 4
Prep 10 mins
Cook 10 mins

500g salmon fillet
40g rolled or porridge oats
juice of ½ lemon
¼ tsp garlic granules or powder
handful of fresh dill or parsley
¼ tsp chilli flakes

Extras
salad leaves
lemon wedges
vegan mayo

1. Firstly, skin the salmon fillet and chop into cubes.

2. Add to a food processor along with the oats, lemon juice, garlic granules, herbs, chilli flakes and a pinch of salt and pepper and pulse until the mixture starts to stick together.

3. Shape into 4 burgers, place on a hot griddle pan and cook on both sides for 5 minutes each.

4. Serve in a bun as a burger or with salad leaves, lemon wedges and vegan mayo.

FAQ

Can I bake them instead? Sure, bake at 200°C/180°C fan/gas 6 for 15 minutes.

Can you cook them on the BBQ? Yes, give it a try in the summer.

Is there a swap for oats? Simply swap with breadcrumbs.

Can you use other fish? Yes, try cod instead.

SIMPLE SAUSAGE, ONION & APPLE TRAYBAKE

This is probably the easiest dinner recipe in the book. It's a favourite of mine when short on time as it only takes 5 minutes to prep.

Serves 2–3
Prep 5 mins
Cook 40 mins

2 red onions
2 apples
400g new potatoes
6 sausages of choice
    (I use meat-free)
1 tbsp fennel seeds
2 tbsp olive oil

1. Preheat the oven to 220°C/200°C fan/gas 7.

2. Cut the onions into quarters, slice the apples around the core into wedges and the baby potatoes in halves.

3. Now, add them all to a large baking tray along with the sausages, fennel seeds, olive oil and some salt and pepper and mix with your hands until well combined.

4. Bake for 20 minutes.

5. Turn the sausages and bake for a further 20 minutes.

FAQ

Would herbs work instead of fennel seeds? Sure, try oregano or basil.

Could I use sweet potato instead? Absolutely, just slice into cubes and follow the same instructions.

SMOKY SAUSAGE & BEAN STEW

Smoky in flavour and packed with sausages and beans, this hearty one-pot stew is one of my favourite dinners during the colder months.

Serves 4
Prep 5 mins
Cook 30 mins

1 red onion
2 tbsp olive oil
4 garlic cloves
2 tsp smoked paprika
2 tsp ground coriander
1 tin (400g) cannellini beans
1 tin (400g) kidney beans
2 × 400g tins chopped tomatoes
1 tbsp tomato purée
1 tbsp maple syrup or honey
6 sausages of choice
   (I use meat-free)

1. Preheat the oven to 220°C/200°C fan/gas 7.

2. Roughly chop the red onion, put in a large ovenproof pan or dish with the oil and place over a medium heat.

3. Add in the crushed garlic, paprika and coriander and cook down for 2–3 minutes until the onion softens.

4. Now, add the drained tinned beans, tinned tomatoes, ¼ tin of water (use the tomato tin), the tomato purée and maple syrup or honey and stir.

5. Bring to the boil, add the sausages and place in the oven to bake, lid off, for 20–25 minutes.

FAQ

Can I just simmer it on the hob rather than baking? Sure, simmer over a low heat for 20 minutes.

Can I use other beans? Sure, use whatever beans you have or prefer.

STICKY SESAME STIR-FRY

An incredible sticky sesame sauce that can be used with any veg you want. It will be the only stir-fry sauce you'll need!

Serves 2
Prep 5 mins
Cook 10 mins

1 green pepper
1 red pepper
150g green beans
1 tbsp oil
70g (½ cup) cashews

Sauce
3 tbsp tamari
2 tbsp maple syrup or runny
   honey
2 tbsp sesame seeds
1 tbsp plain flour
   (I use gluten-free)
juice of 1 lime
pinch of chilli flakes
1 garlic clove

1. Firstly, thinly slice the peppers and chop the ends off the green beans.

2. Heat a wok or frying pan with the oil until hot, then add the peppers, green beans and cashews and fry them together for 7–8 minutes.

3. Meanwhile, add all the sauce ingredients to a jar with the crushed garlic, screw on the lid and shake.

4. Turn the heat off, quickly pour in the sauce and stir it through until it becomes sticky and ready to serve.

FAQ

Not gluten-free? You can swap the tamari for soy sauce.

Can I add extra protein? Sure, add in chicken, prawns or tofu when you stir in the peppers etc.

Nut allergy? Simply avoid using the cashews.

Don't have a jar? Just mix the sauce together in a bowl.

Don't have this veg? You can use the sauce recipe and adjust to use any veg you already have in the fridge.

SWEET POTATO & CHICKPEA CURRY

This brings back memories as it was the first curry I taught myself to cook when I was struggling with my health. It became a recipe I cooked all the time because you can batch cook portions for another day.

Serves 4
Prep 5 mins
Cook 1 hour 5 mins

2 medium sweet potatoes
1 tbsp oil
2 garlic cloves
2 tsp ground turmeric
pinch of chilli flakes
½ tsp paprika
½ tsp cayenne pepper
2 × 400ml tins full-fat coconut milk
2 × 400g tins chopped tomatoes
1 tin (400g) chickpeas
2 large handfuls of spinach or kale

1. Preheat the oven to 220°C/200°C fan/gas 7.

2. Chop the sweet potatoes into cubes (you can leave the skin on as it saves time and reduces waste).

3. Now, heat a large pan over a low/medium heat with the oil and crushed garlic until the garlic begins to sizzle. Add the spices and chopped sweet potato.

4. Pour in the coconut milk, tinned tomatoes and drained chickpeas and stir.

5. Bring to a boil and then cook in the oven, without a lid, for 1 hour.

6. Remove from the oven, add the spinach/kale and stir through until it wilts. Season with salt and pepper.

FAQ

Can I cook on the hob instead? Yes, on a low simmer for 45 minutes–1 hour until you reach the desired consistency.

Don't have sweet potatoes? Swap for butternut squash or white potatoes.

Can you freeze it? Yes, just allow it to cool and then freeze leftovers for another day.

Is it spicy? No, I try to make all my curries mild, so if you like it spicy, I would double/treble the cayenne pepper and chilli flakes.

MISO-GLAZED SALMON KEBABS

The easiest and tastiest fish kebabs I have ever tried. Rich in flavour, these will totally impress the whole family!

Serves 4
Prep 15 mins–1 hour
Cook 15 mins

1 tbsp miso paste
1 tbsp maple syrup or runny
    honey
1 tsp garlic granules or powder
    or 1 crushed garlic clove
3 tbsp water
500g salmon fillet

1. To a small bowl, add the miso paste, maple syrup or honey, garlic and water and mix together.

2. Skin the salmon, chop into cubes and add to the marinade. Stir so the salmon is completely covered.

3. Allow to marinate in the fridge for as long as possible. Try for at least 15 minutes but 1 hour is even better.

4. Preheat the oven to 200°C/180°C fan/gas 6.

5. Push the salmon onto skewers (if you're using wooden ones, soak in water for 10 minutes first so they don't burn). Place on a baking tray lined with baking paper.

6. Bake for 15 minutes.

FAQ

Can I cook these on the hob or BBQ?
Yes, you can fry them in a griddle pan or on the BBQ in the summer.

Vegan? Swap for tofu instead and use maple syrup.

Can I use other meat or fish?
Yes, you could also try it with chicken or a different fish such as cod.

BUTTERNUT SQUASH & COURGETTE BAKED BASMATI RICE

An incredibly easy, comforting one-pot baked rice dish packed full of veg and flavour. It's definitely one you will make time and time again.

Serves 4
Prep 15 mins
Cook 1 hour

4 garlic cloves
1 red onion
1 courgette
2 tbsp olive oil
200g baby plum tomatoes
½ small (300g) butternut squash
1 tbsp paprika
1 tbsp dried fennel seeds
1 tbsp dried basil
350g brown basmati rice
1 litre (4 cups) veg stock
juice of 1 lemon
fresh parsley, to serve (optional)

1. Preheat the oven to 220°C/200°C fan/gas 7.

2. Crush the garlic, roughly slice the onion and chop the courgette and add to a large shallow casserole dish with the oil, whole tomatoes, cubed butternut squash (no need to peel), spices, basil and a pinch of salt and pepper and mix together.

3. Place in the oven for 15 minutes.

4. Remove from the oven and stir in the rice, veg stock and lemon juice. Place back in the oven for 40–45 minutes, without a lid, stirring again after 20 minutes, until the stock has been absorbed.

5. Serve straight to the table topped with fresh parsley, if using.

FAQ

What can I do with leftovers? Allow it to cool and store in a sealed container in the fridge for up to 2 days. I absolutely love this dish cold in a lunch box the next day or you can reheat, but make sure it's piping hot!

Can I use other veg? Absolutely, you can adjust it to use whatever veg you want.

THE BEST GLUTEN-FREE PIZZA

If you're like me and get upset when you go out and order a gluten-free pizza that turns up half the size of your friends', then this is for you! The large base is ready in just 10 minutes for your favourite toppings.

Serves 3
Prep 10 mins
Cook 20 mins

Dough
500g self-raising flour
    (I use gluten-free), plus
    extra for shaping
400g coconut yoghurt
1 tbsp olive oil, plus extra
    for brushing
pinch of salt

Pizza toppings
125g passata
1 tsp dried basil
1 tsp dried oregano
150g grated cheese of choice
    (I use vegan)
3 mushrooms
handful of tomatoes
3 tsp pesto (try my Easy Peasy
    Pesto on page 152) (optional)

1. Line a large pizza or baking tray with baking paper and preheat the oven to 220°C/200°C fan/gas 7.

2. Add the flour, yoghurt, olive oil and salt to a large bowl and mix together with a fork until it starts to stick together.

3. Flour your hands and shape the dough into a large ball.

4. Place onto the pizza tray and either roll out or press down to fill the tray. If your hands are sticking, slightly dampen them.

5. To create the crust, simply pinch in an inch from the edge so it creates more height. You are aiming for the base to be 1cm thick and the crust to be 2cm thick.

6. Brush the crust with olive oil to help it brown when baked.

7. Mix together the passata, basil and oregano, then spread over the pizza, sprinkle with the grated cheese and top with the sliced mushrooms, halved tomatoes and a few spoons of pesto, if using.

8. Bake for 20 minutes until golden.

FAQ

Can I use plain flour instead?
Yes, but the dough won't be quite as fluffy. Simply add 3 tsp baking powder to the mix.

Which yoghurt works best? Go for one that is fairly runny (I use coconut).

STORE CUPBOARD DINNERS

3-BEAN CHILLI

10-MINUTE PEANUT BUTTER CURRY

CHICKPEA & AVOCADO SMASH BURGERS

LAZY LENTIL RAGU

MIXED BEAN STEW

SPEEDY SPINACH & CASHEW 'RICOTTA' PASTA

SWEET POTATO DHAL

TOMATO SOUP

Healthy, affordable dinners you can make using ingredients you probably already have at home. What I love about this chapter is how you will only need two or three fresh ingredients per recipe, meaning you can just grab a few items on your way home from work and pull the rest from your cupboards.

3-BEAN CHILLI

A comforting dinner that you can make completely from the store cupboard. This will totally hit the spot on those colder evenings.

Serves 4
Prep 5 mins
Cook 20 mins

glug of oil
3 garlic cloves
1 tin (400g) butter beans
1 tin (400g) borlotti beans
1 tin (400g) kidney beans
1 tin (200g) sweetcorn
1 tbsp paprika
1 tbsp ground coriander
½ tsp cayenne pepper
large pinch of chilli flakes
1 tsp ground cinnamon
2 tbsp cacao powder
1 jar (680g) passata

1. Add a glug of oil to a large pan over a medium heat, crush the garlic directly into the pan and fry for a minute.

2. Meanwhile, drain and rinse all the beans and sweetcorn in a colander.

3. Add the beans and sweetcorn to the pan along with all the spices, cacao powder, passata and a generous pinch of salt and pepper and stir.

4. Place the lid on and simmer for 15 minutes.

5. Serve with a spoon of yoghurt if you have some in your fridge.

FAQ

What do you serve it with? Try it with rice or quinoa.

Can I freeze it? Absolutely, freeze leftovers for another day.

Can I use other beans? Sure, you can use whichever beans you have or prefer.

Why add cacao powder and is it essential? No, it's not essential but it adds a lovely depth of flavour and colour, so make sure to try it!

Is it spicy? I make all my dishes mild to accommodate all, so by all means spice it up to suit your taste buds.

10-MINUTE PEANUT BUTTER CURRY

This is the most popular curry I have created to date, so I just had to include it in this book! It's a true fan favourite and one that I recommend to anyone when they ask which recipe to try first!

Serves 4
Prep 2 mins
Cook 8 mins

1 red onion
2 large garlic cloves
2 tbsp oil
1 tsp paprika
½ tsp ground coriander
½ tsp cayenne pepper
pinch of chilli flakes
1 tin (400ml) full-fat coconut milk
4 tbsp peanut butter (crunchy
   or smooth)
2 tbsp tomato purée
2 × 400g tins chickpeas
1 tsp veg stock powder
   (or ½ stock cube)
juice of 1 lime

Extras
rice
lime wedges

1. Firstly, prepare the red onion by roughly dicing and crush the garlic.

2. Heat a large pan with the oil, add the crushed garlic and red onion and cook for a minute until slightly softened.

3. Now, add the spices and stir.

4. Finally, add the coconut milk, peanut butter, tomato purée, drained chickpeas, veg stock powder and lime juice and stir.

5. Cook on a high heat for 5–6 minutes until it starts to thicken.

6. Serve with rice and wedges of lime.

FAQ

Peanut allergy? Swap for almond butter.

Can I add extra veg? Absolutely, this is the base of the curry so you could add in whatever veg you want, such as broccoli, spinach and sweet potato.

Is it spicy? No, all my curries are mild to cater for all, so if you prefer spicy curries, I would double/treble the chilli flakes and cayenne pepper.

Nut allergy? Just leave out the peanut butter and make it without – it's still a tasty chickpea curry.

CHICKPEA & AVOCADO SMASH BURGERS

Chickpeas are one of my favourite ingredients and I always have them in the cupboard, so I just had to create a veggie burger using them.

Makes 4
Prep 5 mins
Cook 20 mins
Cool 5 mins

2 × 400g tins chickpeas
1 tbsp smoked paprika
1 tbsp ground coriander
½ tsp garlic granules or powder
2 tbsp tomato purée
juice of 2 limes
1 tbsp olive oil
1 avocado

Extras
buns (I use gluten-free)
vegan mayo
lettuce

1. Preheat the oven to 220°C/200°C fan/gas 7.

2. Drain and rinse the chickpeas, add to a large bowl and mash thoroughly with a potato masher or fork.

3. Add the spices, garlic granules, tomato purée, juice of 1 of the limes, olive oil and a generous pinch of salt and pepper and mix.

4. Shape into 4 patties, place on a baking tray lined with baking paper and bake for 20 minutes.

5. Meanwhile, peel the avocado and add to a bowl along with the juice of the other lime and a generous pinch of salt and pepper. Mash together with a fork.

6. Remove the burgers from the oven and allow to cool for 5 minutes (this helps them to firm up).

7. Serve in buns (gluten-free if you want) with a spreading of vegan mayo, some lettuce and the avocado smash.

FAQ

Any swap for the chickpeas? Try a white bean such as butter beans.

Can I make it oil free? Yes, just add water instead of the olive oil.

Can I freeze them? Sure, freeze once cooked and cooled.

LAZY LENTIL RAGU

Lentils are a great affordable way of making meat-free versions of your favourite classic dishes such as this ragu, which only takes 10 minutes to prepare!

Serves 6
Prep 10 mins
Cook 30 mins

1 onion (red or white)
3 garlic cloves
2 large carrots
3 celery stalks
glug of oil
2 × 400g tins green lentils
1 tin (400g) chopped tomatoes
2 tsp veg stock powder
    (or ½ stock cube)
1 tbsp dried basil
1 tbsp dried oregano
1 tsp dried thyme
3 bay leaves
1 tbsp tamari
140g (1 cup) peas
pasta (I use gluten-free),
    rice or quinoa, to serve

1. Firstly, finely chop the onion, garlic, carrots and celery stalks.

2. Add to a pan on a medium heat with a glug of oil and a pinch of salt and pepper and fry together for 5 minutes until the veg starts to soften.

3. Meanwhile, drain the lentils and add to the pan along with the tinned tomatoes, veg stock powder, herbs, tamari and peas and stir.

4. Simmer on a medium heat for 25 minutes until the ragu thickens, making sure to stir every 10 minutes.

5. Serve with your choice of pasta, rice or quinoa.

FAQ

Can I freeze leftovers? Absolutely, allow the ragu to cool and freeze for another day.

Not gluten-free? Swap tamari for soy sauce or just leave it out.

MIXED BEAN STEW

My favourite way of using up those tinned beans lying around in the back of the cupboard. I love using mixed beans as they're an easy and affordable way of packing plant-based protein into your diet.

Serves 4–6
Prep 5 mins
Cook 40 mins
Cool 5 mins

1 red onion
3 garlic cloves
2 large carrots
2 celery stalks
glug of oil
1 tbsp paprika
1 tbsp ground coriander
1 tin (400g) black beans
1 tin (400g) cannellini beans
1 tin (400g) kidney beans
1 tsp dried thyme
1 tsp dried basil
2 × 400g tins chopped tomatoes
2 tsp veg stock powder
  (or 1 stock cube)

1. Preheat the oven to 220°C/200°C fan/gas 7.

2. Dice the red onion, crush the garlic, roughly chop the carrots and celery and add all to a large pan with a glug of oil and the spices and fry together for 5–6 minutes.

3. Meanwhile, drain and rinse the beans and add to the pan with the herbs, tinned tomatoes, 1 tin of water (use the tomato tin) and veg stock powder and stir.

4. Bring to a boil and cook in the oven for 30 minutes (or just on a low simmer for 25–30 minutes).

5. Remove from the oven, allow to cool for 5 minutes and it's then ready to serve.

FAQ

What to serve it with? I serve it with rice or quinoa but you could totally just eat it on its own.

Can you swap for other beans? Absolutely, you can add in any beans you want or even chickpeas.

Can I add extra veg? Definitely, add in whatever veg you have in the fridge when adding the carrots and celery.

Can you freeze leftovers? Yes, allow to cool then place the stew in containers to freeze for another day.

SPEEDY SPINACH & CASHEW 'RICOTTA' PASTA

This has quickly become my new favourite quick but comforting pasta recipe. Using cashews creates a delicious dairy-free, ricotta-style texture.

Serves 2
Prep 5 mins
Cook 12 mins

250g pasta (I use gluten-free)
200g frozen spinach

Cashew 'ricotta'
125g cashews
juice of ½ lemon
20g (¼ cup) nutritional yeast
¼ tsp garlic granules or powder
    or ½ garlic clove
60ml (¼ cup) cold water
pinch of salt

1. Firstly, add the pasta and spinach to a pan and boil for 10–12 minutes.

2. Meanwhile, put the cashews in a bowl and cover with boiling water for 5 minutes.

3. Drain the cashews and add to a blender with the other 'ricotta' ingredients. Blend until a thick but smooth consistency forms.

4. Once the pasta and spinach have finished cooking, drain in a colander, saving 60ml (¼ cup) of pasta water, and place back into the pan.

5. Add the 'ricotta' sauce along with the saved pasta water and mix until well combined.

FAQ

Can I use fresh spinach? Sure, I would use a 400g bag of fresh spinach and wilt down in the pasta water just before draining.

What is nutritional yeast and where do I buy it? Refer to page 19.

SWEET POTATO DHAL

A delicious mild curry that is packed full of colour and flavour and will taste better than any takeaway.

Serves 4
Prep 5 mins
Cook 30 mins

red or white onion
3 garlic cloves
glug of oil
2 small sweet potatoes or 1 large (500g)
1 tbsp ground turmeric
1 tsp paprika
1 tsp ground coriander
½ tsp chilli flakes
½ tsp cayenne pepper
juice of 1 lime
1 tin (400ml) full-fat coconut milk
1 tsp veg stock powder (or ½ stock cube)
500ml (2 cups) water
180g (1 cup) red split lentils

1. Firstly, dice the onion and crush the garlic. Add to a large pan with a glug of oil and cook over a medium heat for 2 minutes.

2. Meanwhile, peel and chop the sweet potato into very small cubes, adding to the pan as you chop.

3. Stir in all the spices, then pour in the lime juice, coconut milk, veg stock powder, water, lentils and a pinch of salt and pepper and simmer for 20–25 minutes until the sweet potato is cooked through.

FAQ

How spicy is it? If you add just the ½ tsp chilli flakes and cayenne pepper it's on the milder side but if you prefer hot curries, I would double the chilli flakes and cayenne pepper.

Can you freeze it? Absolutely, allow to cool then freeze.

Can I add in extra protein? Sure, you could add in tofu, chicken or even prawns.

TOMATO SOUP

A quick yet comforting tomato soup that's ready in under 15 minutes using one pan and all store cupboard ingredients. No need to spend hours roasting tomatoes!

Serves 2–3
Prep 2–3 mins
Cook 15 mins

1 red onion
2 garlic cloves
glug of oil
1 tbsp dried basil
1 tbsp dried oregano
2 × 400g tins chopped tomatoes
1 tsp veg stock powder
   (or ½ stock cube)

1. Firstly, dice the onion and crush the garlic. Add to a pan with a glug of oil, the basil, oregano and a pinch of salt and pepper and fry for 5 minutes on a medium heat.

2. Now, add the tinned tomatoes, ½ tin of water (use the tomato tin) and veg stock powder and stir.

3. Simmer for 7–8 minutes on a medium heat.

4. Finally, blend until smooth or serve chunky.

FAQ

Don't have tinned tomatoes? Swap for a large jar of passata.

Can you freeze leftovers? Absolutely, allow to cool then freeze.

BATCH COOKING

BLACK BEAN NACHOS

BLACK BEAN TACOS

HOMEMADE SWEET POTATO
GNOCCHI

CHEESY GNOCCHI BAKE

PAN-FRIED PEA GNOCCHI

PESTO BEAN & KALE SALAD

EASY PEASY PESTO RISOTTO

MEAT-FREE BALL PASTA

MEAT-FREE BALL MARINARA SUB

Possibly my favourite chapter in this book. There are four hero recipes that you can make in bulk, which will then turn into three other delicious recipes. This means you can make three different dinners out of one key recipe, which is ideal during a busy week. It's a really smart, fun and creative way of cooking to reduce time in the kitchen.

BLACK BEAN SAUCE

An incredibly simple black bean sauce using store cupboard ingredients, which you can make in 25 minutes. This is great for using in fajitas, enchiladas, for topping nachos or simply serving with rice.

Makes 16 portions
Prep 5 mins
Cook 20 mins

4 red onions
8 garlic cloves
glug of oil
2 tbsp paprika
2 tbsp ground coriander
1 tsp cayenne pepper
2 pinches of chilli flakes
4 × 400g tins black beans
4 × 400g tins chopped tomatoes
2 tbsp tamari (optional)

1. Firstly, roughly dice the onions and crush the garlic cloves.

2. Now, add them to a large pan on a medium heat with a glug of oil along with the spices and fry together for 5 minutes.

3. Finally, add in the drained black beans, tinned tomatoes, tamari and a generous pinch of salt and pepper and simmer for 15 minutes, making sure to stir every few minutes.

FAQ

Can you freeze? Absolutely, simply allow to cool then portion out into Tupperware boxes and freeze for up to 3 months.

Can I store in the fridge? Of course, store in a sealed container in the fridge for up to 3 days.

BLACK BEAN ENCHILADAS

Like a sort of Mexican lasagne, flavour-packed enchiladas
are an easy supper that everyone will love.

Serves: 4
Prep 5 mins
Cook 20 mins

6–8 wraps (I use gluten-free)
6 portions of Black Bean Sauce
(page 134)
150g grated cheese of choice
(I use vegan)
chopped fresh coriander or
parsley, to serve (optional)

1. Preheat the oven to 220°C/200°C fan/gas 7.

2. Add a few spoonfuls of the black bean sauce into each wrap
and roll them up.

3. Place into a large baking dish.

4. Finally, top with more black bean sauce and sprinkle over
the grated cheese.

5. Bake for 20 minutes. Serve with a scattering of herbs,
if wished.

FAQ

Do you have a dip to go with them?
Serve with a side of my Speedy Avocado
Salsa (page 172).

BLACK BEAN NACHOS

The perfect starter, side or main to share. Tortillas topped with my black bean sauce, cheese and served with salsa, this will quickly become a favourite recipe you make time and time again.

Serves 2–4
Prep 5 mins
Cook 12 mins

200g bag of salted tortillas crisps
  (I use gluten-free)
200g grated cheese of choice
  (I use vegan)
1–2 jalapeños, from a jar
2 portions of Black Bean Sauce
  (page 134)

1. Preheat the oven to 220°C/200°C fan/gas 7.

2. Empty half a bag of tortillas into a baking dish/tray. Top with 100g of grated cheese, the sliced jalapeños and 3 heaped spoons of the black bean sauce.

3. Add the rest of the tortillas on top, 3 more heaped spoons of black bean sauce and the leftover grated cheese.

4. Bake for 12 minutes until the cheese has melted and it's golden.

FAQ

Do you have a dip to go with them?
Serve with a side of my Speedy Avocado Salsa (page 172).

BLACK BEAN TACOS

Delicious, meat-free soft tacos for when you fancy a homemade Mexican meal. Ready in under 10 minutes if you have batch cooked the sauce.

Makes 6
Prep 10 mins
Cook 5 mins

6 wraps (I use gluten-free)
2 avocados
handful of fresh coriander
1 red chilli
3 portions of Black Bean Sauce
   (page 134)
coconut yoghurt
1 lime

1. Firstly, heat up your wraps in the oven or microwave.

2. Meanwhile, peel and slice the avocado, roughly chop the coriander and slice the chilli.

3. Finally, add 2 heaped spoons of the warmed-up black bean sauce into the centre of each of the wraps, top with the avocado, coriander, chilli, a dollop of yoghurt and a squeeze of lime juice and serve.

FAQ

Don't like coriander? Serve with fresh parsley instead.

Can't get fresh chilli? Sprinkle in chilli flakes instead.

Can I add in extra ingredients? Of course, you could add in anything you want, such as meat, fish or veg.

HOMEMADE SWEET POTATO GNOCCHI

Making your own gnocchi is surprisingly easy to do. You can batch-make 12 portions and I'll show you how to turn that into three delicious dinners.

Makes 12 portions
Prep 10 mins
Cook 1 hour
Cool 20 mins

1.5kg sweet potatoes
large pinch of salt
500g plain flour
   (I use gluten-free)

1. Preheat the oven to 220°C/200°C fan/gas 7.

2. Slice the sweet potatoes in half, place on a baking tray with the flesh side up and bake for 45 minutes.

3. Remove from the oven and allow to cool for 15–20 minutes.

4. Now, scoop out the sweet potato flesh into a large bowl and mash.

5. Add a large pinch of salt and then mix in the flour with your hands, adding the flour in stages until the dough does not feel wet (you may not need it all).

6. Divide the dough into quarters. Now, with slightly damp hands, take one piece of the dough and roll it in your hands into sausage shapes. Cut each sausage into gnocchi and use a fork to make ridges that will hold the sauce.

7. Once you have made all the pieces (it should be around 120), heat a large pot with water and a pinch of salt until boiling.

8. Carefully add about 20–30 gnocchi pieces at a time and cook until they rise to the top (roughly 3 minutes). Remove with a strainer and place on a plate or a tray lined with kitchen paper to remove excess moisture.

9. Repeat the process with the other gnocchi until all are cooked.

FAQ

Can I store in the fridge? Sure, just allow to cool, place in a sealed container and keep in the fridge for up to 3 days.

Can I freeze the gnocchi? Yes, once boiled allow them to cool and then freeze.

CHEESY GNOCCHI BAKE

Who doesn't love a pasta bake? This gnocchi bake is just as good, if not better! There's no need to cook a separate tomato sauce, everything is made in one dish, ready to bake.

Serves 3
Prep 5 mins
Cook 25 mins

1 red onion
2 garlic cloves
4 portions of Homemade Sweet
   Potato Gnocchi (page 142)
   or 400g shop bought
   (I use gluten-free)
handful of cherry tomatoes
   (100g)
1 tin (400g) chopped tomatoes
1 tsp dried basil
1 tsp dried oregano
100g grated cheese of choice
   (I use vegan)
fresh basil, to serve (optional)

1. Preheat the oven to 220°C/200°C fan/gas 7.

2. Prepare the onion by roughly dicing it and crush the garlic.

3. Add both to a large baking dish along with the cooked gnocchi, tomatoes, tinned tomatoes, basil, oregano, salt and pepper and 50g of the grated cheese. Mix with a spoon.

4. Finally, sprinkle over the remaining 50g of cheese and bake for 25 minutes.

5. Once baked, top with fresh basil, if you wish, and it's ready to serve.

FAQ

What if I am using store-bought gnocchi? That's fine, just boil as per the packet instructions before adding to the baking dish.

GNOCCHI VEGETABLE TRAYBAKE

I love anything that cooks in one pot or tray as it means less washing-up afterwards! Mix up veg of every colour you can here to get maximum nutrition.

Serves 2
Prep 5 mins
Cook 20 mins

1 pepper
1 courgette
1 large red onion
200g cherry tomatoes
3 portions of Homemade Sweet
    Potato Gnocchi (page 142)
2 garlic cloves
1 tsp dried basil
1 tsp dried oregano
3 tbsp oil

1. Preheat your oven to 220°C/200°C fan/gas 7.

2. Roughly chop the vegetables and place into a large baking tray.

3. Add the cooked gnocchi, crushed garlic, basil, oregano and a little salt and pepper and mix together. Drizzle over the oil.

4. Bake for 20 minutes.

FAQ

Can I use store-bought gnocchi?
That's fine, just boil 300g as per the packet instructions before adding to the baking tray.

PAN-FRIED PEA GNOCCHI

A delicious super-quick lunch or dinner that can be made in just 10 minutes. Crispy pan-fried gnocchi is simply the best – you have to try it!

Serves 2
Prep 2 mins
Cook 10 mins

2 tbsp oil
2 portions of Homemade Sweet
    Potato Gnocchi (page 142)
    or 200g store bought
    (I use gluten-free)
1 small red onion
1 garlic clove
140g (1 cup) peas
2 handfuls of kale or spinach

1. To a large pan over a medium heat, add the oil and the cooked gnocchi to fry together for 2–3 minutes.

2. Meanwhile, slice the red onion and crush the garlic and add to the pan along with the peas, kale and some salt and pepper.

3. Fry together for a further 7–8 minutes until the onion softens and the gnocchi is crispy.

FAQ

What if I am using store-bought gnocchi? That's fine, just boil as per the packet instructions before adding to the pan.

Want to go all out? Try adding a few spoons of homemade Easy Peasy Pesto (page 152).

EASY PEASY PESTO

Nothing compares to homemade fresh pesto. This easy batch version makes 15 portions that can be used in so many different ways.

Makes 15 heaped spoons
Prep 5 mins

100g pine nuts
125ml (½ cup) olive oil
100g fresh basil leaves, plus stalks
2 garlic cloves
juice of ½ lemon
generous pinch of salt
50g grated cheese of choice
    (I use vegan)

1. To a food processor, add all the ingredients and pulse into a pesto paste.

2. Add to a jar with a lid and store in the fridge for up to 7 days.

FAQ

Could I freeze it? Absolutely, try freezing in batches or add to an ice-cube tray.

Is there a cheese substitute? Sure, try 2 tablespoons nutritional yeast.

PESTO BEAN & KALE SALAD

Turn your pesto into a super-greens lunch, with added beans to keep you full, in less than 10 minutes.

Makes 2 mains or 4 sides
Prep 10 mins

1 tin (400g) butter beans
1 avocado
150g kale
4 heaped tbsp Easy Peasy Pesto
　　(page 152)
juice of ½ lemon

1. Firstly, drain and rinse the butter beans and peel and chop the avocado.

2. Add the kale, pesto, beans, avocado, lemon juice and a pinch of salt and pepper into a large bowl and gently mix with your hands to soften the kale.

FAQ

What else can I add? Try roasting sweet potato or butternut squash cubes and mixing into the salad.

Don't like kale? Substitute lettuce or rocket leaves.

Don't have butter beans? Simply swap for other white beans, such as cannellini or haricot. You could also swap for chickpeas.

Can I use store-bought pesto? Absolutely.

CRISPY PESTO PASTRY TWISTS

These easy twists are amazing! The perfect starter or snack to make for a party or gathering, they ooze with pesto, are crunchy and totally delicious.

Makes 8
Prep 5 mins
Cook 15 mins

1 gluten-free puff pastry sheet
6 heaped tbsp Easy Peasy Pesto
(page 152)

1. Preheat the oven to 220°C/200°C fan/gas 7.

2. Unroll the pastry sheet and slice in half from the narrowest edge.

3. Add the pesto to one of the sheets and spread it out so that it covers all the pastry. Now, place the empty sheet on top so the pesto is 'sandwiched' between the layers.

4. Slice 4 long strips from the narrowest edge and then cut across the middle so you have 8 equal pieces.

5. Holding the ends of each piece, carefully twist them a couple of times.

6. Spread the twists out on a baking tray lined with baking paper and bake for 15 minutes or until golden.

FAQ

Can I use pre-made pesto instead? Absolutely!

How do you serve them? These are best served warm straight out of the oven but you could also serve them cold before dinner when having guests.

EASY PEASY PESTO RISOTTO

Want to know how I save time and hassle when making a risotto?
Well, I add all the stock at once, so you don't have to keep standing
by the hob adding more every few minutes. We don't have time for that!

Serves 4
Prep 5 mins
Cook 30 mins

1 red onion
1 courgette
glug of oil
140g (1 cup) peas
350g risotto rice
1 tin (400ml) full-fat coconut milk
750ml (3 cups) veg stock
5 heaped tbsp Easy Peasy Pesto
   (page 152)
100g kale or spinach

1. Firstly, roughly dice the onion and chop the courgette into small cubes.

2. Pour the oil into a large casserole dish or frying pan and add the onion, courgette, peas and a pinch of salt and pepper and fry together for 5 minutes.

3. Now, add the risotto rice, coconut milk, veg stock and pesto and stir on a low simmer for 20 minutes until it thickens.

4. Finally, add in the kale and simmer the risotto for roughly 5 minutes until it thickens and the kale has wilted.

FAQ

Could I add extra protein into this?
Sure, at the end you can top with grilled chicken, prawns or tofu, if you wish.

How do I store leftovers? I love cold risotto leftovers the next day. Simply allow the risotto to cool, then immediately place in the fridge in a sealed container. You can also reheat the rice, but make sure it's piping hot!

MEAT-FREE BALLS

This is one of the best recipes for when you're trying to reduce your meat consumption but are still craving the family favourites.

Makes 20 balls
Prep 10 mins
Cook 20 mins
Cool 15 mins

200g chestnut mushrooms
1 red onion
3 garlic cloves
1 tin (400g) black beans
couple of glugs of oil
50g walnuts
2 tbsp tamari
80g (1 cup) porridge oats
1 tbsp dried basil
1 tbsp dried oregano

1. Firstly, chop the mushrooms into small pieces, dice the onion, crush the garlic and drain the tin of black beans.

2. Pour a glug of oil into a pan over a medium heat. Add in the red onion, garlic and mushrooms, then the black beans, walnuts and tamari and fry for 5–7 minutes until the liquid has disappeared.

3. Now, add the mixture to a food processor along with the oats, basil, oregano and a generous pinch of salt and pepper. Pulse the mixture to combine until the texture is like stuffing (you may need to scrape down the sides a few times).

4. Place the food processor with the mixture into the fridge for 10–15 minutes to take away some of the heat.

5. Roll into roughly 20 small meatballs.

6. Reheat the pan with another glug of oil over a low heat, add in the meatballs and fry for 10 minutes, making sure to shake the pan so that they fry all the way round.

FAQ

Can I freeze them? Yes, once you have pan-fried them just allow to cool then freeze.

Not gluten-free? Use soy sauce instead of tamari.

Can I bake them instead? Yes, add to a baking tray lined with baking paper and bake at 180°C/160°C fan/gas 4 for 20 minutes.

MEAT-FREE BALL PASTA

A plant-based version of a true classic! Protein-packed balls cooked in my go-to speedy tomato sauce.

Serves 2
Prep 2 mins
Cook 15 mins

2 tbsp olive oil
250g cherry or baby plum tomatoes
200g pasta (I use gluten-free)
2 garlic cloves
4 tbsp tomato purée
juice of 1 lemon
1 tsp paprika
pinch of chilli flakes
6–8 Meat-Free Balls (page 160)
fresh basil (optional)

1. Heat the oil in a frying pan, add the whole baby tomatoes and fry over a medium heat for 7–8 minutes until they soften.

2. Place your pasta in boiling water and boil for 10 minutes.

3. With a fork, gently press the tomatoes until they burst.

4. Now, crush the garlic into the pan and add the tomato purée, lemon juice, paprika, chilli flakes and a pinch of black pepper. Mix and simmer for 7–8 minutes.

5. Spoon your meat-free balls into the pan along with the cooked and drained pasta and mix through until well combined.

6. Finally, top with fresh basil, if using, and serve.

FAQ

Can I use a tin of tomatoes or passata instead? Sure, swap the fresh tomatoes for 1 tin (400g) tomatoes or 400g passata. You will need to simmer down for a little longer though to reach the desired consistency.

Not meat-free? Simply swap for meatballs of your choice.

MEAT-FREE BALLS WITH PEA & PARSLEY MASH

If you haven't tried meatballs, mash and gravy, you've been missing out! This greens-infused mash goes perfectly with my meat-free balls.

Serves 4
Prep 5 mins
Cook 15 mins

1kg potatoes
280g (2 cups) peas
handful of fresh parsley
125ml (½ cup) milk of choice
2 knobs of butter (I use vegan)
12–16 Meat-Free Balls (page 160)
Red Onion Gravy (page 180)

1. Chop the potatoes into rough cubes and add to a large pot of boiling salted water along with the peas. Boil for 12 minutes until the potatoes soften.

2. Once boiled, drain the potatoes and peas and add back to the pot along with the chopped parsley, milk, butter and a generous pinch of salt and pepper. Mash until the potato is smooth.

3. Serve with the hot meat-free balls and red onion gravy.

FAQ

Can I freeze leftover mash? Yes, simply allow to cool and freeze into portions for another day.

What else can I do with leftover mash? You can turn it into potato patties by mixing through flour to bind and spices to flavour, then shaping into patties and frying or baking until golden.

MEAT-FREE BALL MARINARA SUB

Hands down my favourite baguette, wrap or sandwich filler.

Serves 2
Prep 2 mins
Cook 10 mins

1 tbsp oil
1 garlic clove
1 tsp dried basil
250g (1 cup) passata
6 Meat-Free Balls (page 160)
baguette, bread or wraps,
    to serve (I use gluten-free)
fresh basil, to serve (optional)

1. Pour the oil into a small pan, add the crushed garlic and dried basil and fry for 1–2 minutes over a medium heat.

2. Now, add the passata, salt and pepper and meat-free balls and simmer for 5 minutes.

3. Serve in a baguette, sandwich or wrap topped with chopped fresh basil.

FAQ

If I am meal-prepping this, when should I add the meatballs and sauce? Try to add them as late as possible to stop the sauce softening the bread. If that's not possible, then it will still be fine.

SIDES

SPEEDY AVOCADO SALSA

CHEESY GARLIC DOUGH BALLS

RED ONION GRAVY

RED ONION HUMMUS

SALT & VINEGAR SMASHED POTATOES

BATTERED TOFU NUGGETS

WOK-FRIED GREENS

CASHEW 'PARMESAN'

VANILLA CASHEW CREAM

Sides are a quick and easy way to increase your daily portions of healthy vegetables simply by adding them as an accompaniment to your meals. Here you will find my favourite vegetable sides and a couple of delicious sauces to accompany a lot of recipes in the book. There are also a few recipes that those who are gluten-free may have missed out on until now.

SPEEDY AVOCADO SALSA

An amazing summer BBQ side dish or for those homemade Mexican nights in.

Serves 4
Prep 10 mins

200g baby plum tomatoes
1 ripe avocado
handful of fresh coriander
juice of 1 lime
1 tsp paprika
pinch of chilli flakes

1. Firstly, chop the tomatoes into quarters, peel and chop the avocado into small cubes and roughly chop the fresh coriander, adding all to a large bowl.

2. Add the juice of a lime, paprika, chilli flakes and a pinch of salt and mix together.

FAQ

Is it spicy? No, the spice is there for flavouring but you could add more chilli flakes if you prefer it hot.

How long will it last? Store in a sealed container in the fridge for up to 2 days.

What shall I serve it with? Try this with the nachos recipe on page 138, enchiladas on page 136 or tacos on page 140.

CHEESY GARLIC DOUGH BALLS

Using the same dough as the flatbread (page 178), you can easily make the most delicious gluten-free dough balls with only 10 minutes of preparation!

Makes 6
Prep 10 mins
Cook 20 mins

Dough
200g self-raising flour
   (I use gluten-free)
180g coconut yoghurt
1 tsp oil
pinch of salt

Cheesy garlic
50g cheese of choice
   (I use vegan)
35g butter (I use vegan)
2 garlic cloves
small handful of fresh parsley

1. Preheat the oven to 220°C/200°C fan/gas 7.

2. To a large bowl, add the flour, yoghurt, oil and a pinch of salt and mix together until well combined.

3. Chop the cheese into 6 small cubes.

4. Slightly dampen your hands, grab a small handful of the dough and flatten it out. Place the cheese cube in the middle, fold the dough around it and roll into a ball. Repeat until all 6 balls are rolled.

5. Now, in a small pan, heat the butter, crushed garlic and finely chopped parsley until the butter is melted.

6. Brush the balls with the melted butter, place onto a baking tray lined with baking paper and bake for 15 minutes.

FAQ

Can you make these without the cheese? Absolutely, just roll into balls without stuffing them.

Can you make these without the garlic butter? Yes, just brush with olive oil before baking.

Can I use a different yoghurt? Sure, I used an unsweetened coconut yoghurt but any other plain yoghurts such as soya would work too.

When are these best served? Straight out of the oven! But you could serve them once cooled if you wish.

MISO & SESAME ROASTED AUBERGINE

This miso sauce has an amazing umami flavour and is the easiest way to upgrade your aubergines to a whole new level of deliciousness.

Serves 2
Prep 2 mins
Cook 30 mins

1 aubergine
1 tbsp miso paste
1 tbsp maple syrup or honey
1 tbsp sesame seeds
1 tbsp water

1. Preheat the oven to 220°C/200°C fan/gas 7.

2. Slice the aubergine in half lengthways and slice deep slits across the flesh side.

3. Place on a baking tray, flesh side facing up, and bake for 20 minutes.

4. Meanwhile, in a small bowl mix the miso paste, maple syrup or honey, sesame seeds and water until smooth.

5. Remove the aubergines from the oven and coat with the sauce, making sure to get the sauce deep down into the aubergine slits.

6. Place back in the oven and bake for a further 10 minutes.

FAQ

What do you serve it with? I love keeping it simple and serving with noodles or rice, to top salads or even chopped up in wraps or sandwiches.

How long will it last? Store in a sealed container in the fridge for up to 3 days.

GARLIC BUTTER FLATBREAD

The same no-prove dough that I use to make my pizza, but here turned into the most amazing starter or side to share.

Serves 4
Prep 10 mins
Cook 20 mins

Dough
250g self-raising flour
(I use gluten-free)
200g coconut yoghurt
1 tsp oil
pinch of salt

Garlic butter
35g butter (I use vegan)
2 garlic cloves
small handful of fresh parsley

1. Preheat the oven to 220°C/200°C fan/gas 7 and line a baking or pizza tray with baking paper.

2. To a large bowl, add the flour, yoghurt, oil and a pinch of salt and mix together until well combined.

3. Shape into a large ball and add to the baking tray, then press down into an oval shape, roughly 1–1.5cm thick. Make sure to press in around the edges to stop any spills.

4. To create a crust, push the middle in so it's a little thinner, which will help to make a raised crust edge.

5. Now, in a small pan heat the butter, crushed garlic and finely chopped parsley until the butter is melted.

6. Pour the garlic butter into the middle of the flatbread and gently brush it to cover.

7. Bake for 15 minutes or until golden.

FAQ

Can I use a different yoghurt? Sure, any unsweetened yoghurt should work.

Could you use this dough to make other recipes? Absolutely, I use this to make 2 quick homemade Naans. Follow the same method, but just leave out the butter topping, shape and then either bake or dry-fry in a large hot non-stick pan.

Can you make it without the garlic butter? Absolutely, just glaze with olive oil before baking.

Would other toppings work? Yes, try topping with my Easy Peasy Pesto (page 152) before baking.

RED ONION GRAVY

A rich vegan gravy that you can make in just 20 minutes. Pour this over the Meat-Free Balls with Pea & Parsley Mash (page 164) or the Mushroom & Lentil Wellington (page 88) for the perfect Sunday roast.

Serves 6–8
Prep 5 mins
Cook 15 mins

2 large red onions
2 garlic cloves
glug of oil
2 tbsp plain flour
    (I use gluten-free)
500ml (2 cups) veg stock
1 tbsp tamari
1 tbsp cacao powder

1. Finely slice the onion and crush the garlic. Put in a large deep frying pan with a glug of oil and a pinch of salt.

2. Fry for 10 minutes over a medium heat, making sure to stir every few minutes.

3. Once the onions are browning and have softened, add the flour and mix it through for a few minutes.

4. Finally, add the veg stock, tamari and cacao powder and mix together.

5. Simmer for 5 minutes until the gravy thickens.

FAQ

Why add cacao powder? It adds a lovely depth of flavour, plus gives a great colour to the gravy.

Can you freeze it? Absolutely, just allow it to cool then freeze it to use another day.

RED ONION HUMMUS

A simple, flavour-packed smooth hummus with caramelised onions that will totally impress. Serve up as a dip with veg crudités or add into sandwiches or wraps.

Serves 6
Prep 15 mins
Cook 10 mins

1 large red onion
5 tbsp olive oil, plus extra
    for drizzling
1 tin (400g) chickpeas
1 tbsp tahini
1 garlic clove
juice of 1 lemon
small handful of fresh parsley
    (optional)

1. Firstly, finely slice the red onion and put it into a frying pan along with 2 tablespoons of the olive oil and a generous pinch of salt.

2. Fry over a medium heat for 10 minutes until the onions are going golden and soft, making sure to stir every few minutes.

3. Meanwhile, into a food processor add the drained chickpeas, remaining olive oil, tahini, crushed garlic, lemon juice and most of the fresh parsley and blend until smooth.

4. Take the onions off the heat and add half to the hummus, pulsing again until blended.

5. Serve in a bowl and top with the rest of the onion, a drizzle of oil and a scattering of the remaining chopped parsley.

FAQ

How long will this last? Store in a sealed container in the fridge for up to 3 days.

Can I make it even creamier? Sure, just add a little more oil when blending.

What shall I serve it with? Try this in the Grilled Pressed Wrap on page 60 or use for dipping the Falafels on page 58 or Garlic Butter Flatbread on page 178.

SALT & VINEGAR SMASHED POTATOES

These crispy smashed potatoes are one of my favourite sides and go with so many different dishes. Once you try them, you'll be hooked!

Serves 4
Prep 5 mins
Cook 45 mins

1kg new potatoes
8 tbsp cider vinegar
6 tbsp olive oil

1. Firstly, add the new potatoes to a pot and cover with hot water from the tap. Add 2 tablespoons of the cider vinegar and a generous pinch of salt and bring to the boil for 15 minutes. Cook until the potatoes are soft when a fork goes through them.

2. Meanwhile, preheat your oven to 220°C/200°C fan/gas 7 and line a baking tray with baking paper.

3. Pour the olive oil and remaining cider vinegar into a bowl and mix together.

4. Drain the potatoes, add to the baking tray and gently press each with a fork until they break apart.

5. Pour over the oil and vinegar mixture, making sure to cover all the potatoes. Scatter over a generous few pinches of salt.

6. Bake for 30 minutes until golden brown.

FAQ

Could I use other vinegars? Yes, any vinegar should work.

How long will these last? They will only be crunchy when used that day, but you can store them in the fridge for up to 3 days in a sealed container.

BATTERED TOFU NUGGETS

Golden, crispy, meat-free nuggets – a brilliant side dish or starter when you're hosting family or friends.

Serves 4
Prep 15 mins
Cook 5 mins

400g firm tofu
500ml (2 cups) sunflower oil
100g plain flour (I use gluten-free)
½ tsp paprika
½ tsp ground turmeric
½ tsp garlic granules or powder
1 tsp baking powder
185ml (¾ cup) sparkling water

1. Firstly, drain and press the tofu block for 10 minutes.

2. Heat the oil in a wok or large pot over a medium heat. You can check it's up to temperature by dipping a wooden spoon into the oil. When it starts to show bubbles around the spoon, it's ready to fry.

3. Meanwhile, prepare the batter. Add the flour, paprika, turmeric, garlic, baking powder, a pinch of salt and pepper and the sparkling water to a large bowl and whisk into a smooth batter.

4. Pull apart the tofu into chunks and dip into the batter so they are completely covered. Carefully lower into the oil using a slotted spoon and fry for 5 minutes or until golden.

5. Remove onto a plate lined with kitchen paper to absorb the leftover oil.

6. Serve in a bowl with a scattering of salt.

FAQ

What would you serve them with? They go really well dipped into mayonnaise.

Can I bake them instead? Unfortunately not, the batter won't go crispy in the same way.

Can I make this with chicken instead? Sure, just follow the same steps but with cubed chicken, frying until cooked right through.

WOK-FRIED GREENS

I love adding extra greens to my dinners and this is my
go-to side dish, which is so easy and tasty!

Serves 4 as a side
Prep 2 mins
Cook 10 mins

1 garlic clove
1 tbsp oil
200g long-stem broccoli
2 pak choi
150g green beans
2 tbsp tamari
1 tbsp maple syrup or runny
  honey
1 tbsp sesame seeds

1. Firstly, roughly slice the garlic.

2. Heat a wok with the oil and when hot, add in the garlic and greens and fry for 5 minutes.

3. Now add the tamari, maple syrup or honey and the sesame seeds and fry for a further 5 minutes.

FAQ

Not gluten-free? Swap the tamari for soy sauce.

Don't have a wok? Simply fry in a large non-stick pan instead.

CASHEW 'PARMESAN'

A simple vegan alternative to Parmesan, perfect for sprinkling over pasta or pizza. The flavour this creates will surprise you.

Makes 18 portions (1 tbsp per serving)
Prep 5 mins

125g cashews
20g (¼ cup) nutritional yeast
¼ tsp garlic granules or powder
generous pinch of salt

1. Add all the ingredients to a small food processor or blender and blend until a crumb texture is formed.

FAQ

How long will it last? Store in a sealed container in the fridge for up to 3 weeks.

What is nutritional yeast and where do I buy it? See page 19.

Which recipes can I use it with? Try using it to top the Speedy Spinach & Cashew 'Ricotta' Pasta (page 124) or No-Chop Bolognese (page 92).

VANILLA CASHEW CREAM

This cashew cream is the real deal. Being dairy-free doesn't mean you have to miss out on cream. It goes incredibly well spooned or poured over a lot of desserts in this book!

Serves 8
Prep 12 mins

150g cashews
2 tbsp maple syrup or runny honey
1 tsp vanilla extract
125ml (½ cup) milk of choice

1. Firstly, place the cashews into a bowl or the cup of a blender and cover with boiling water. Allow to soak for 10 minutes.

2. Drain the cashews and add back to the blender cup along with the maple syrup or honey, vanilla extract and milk and blend for roughly 2 minutes until it reaches a creamy, thick consistency.

FAQ

Can I make a thinner cream? Yes, this makes a wonderful pouring cream for desserts like my Apple & Berry Oat Crumble (page 200). Just use more milk – about 185ml (¾ cup).

How long will this last? You can store it in the fridge for up to 3 days (it will thicken the longer you leave it, so you may need to blend it with a little more milk before using).

What recipes is it good with? It's amazing with quite a few of my desserts in this book. Try it spooned over the chocolate tart (page 210), brownies (page 204) or muffins (page 208).

Is there a nut-free version of this? Unfortunately not as the cashews give it the creamy texture.

DESSERTS

EASY CHOCOLATE GANACHE

APPLE & BERRY OAT CRUMBLE

BLUEBERRY GALETTES

CHOCOLATE BROWNIES

PEANUT BUTTER BANANA BREAD

DOUBLE-CHOCOLATE MUFFINS

NO-BAKE CHOCOLATE TART

UPSIDE-DOWN LEMON CAKE

GOOEY NUT-BUTTER CHOC POT

Incredibly easy desserts for all occasions that everyone will love. I've created healthier twists for some of your favourite desserts and added in some new ones, plus they are all totally gluten, dairy, egg and refined sugar free to help cater for all.

EASY CHOCOLATE GANACHE

A decadent ganache with a surprise ingredient that takes cakes, cupcakes and brownies to the next level.

Serves 9
Prep 5 mins
Cool 20–30 mins

1 large or 2 small ripe avocados
40g cacao powder
6 tbsp maple syrup or runny
    honey

1. Simply peel and de-stone the avocados, then add to a small food processor.

2. Add the cacao powder, maple syrup or honey and a pinch of salt and blend until a smooth ganache forms, scraping down the sides if needed to ensure all the avocado is blended in.

3. If you have time, place the ganache in the fridge for 20–30 minutes to help it firm up slightly.

FAQ

How can I use this? Try it as a topping for my brownies (page 204) or chocolate muffins (page 208), add into the middle of tiered cakes or you could even just use it as a chocolate dip!

APPLE & BERRY OAT CRUMBLE

Crumbles are one of my favourite desserts and when I experimented with oats instead of flour for the topping, it worked incredibly well, so this is now the only crumble I make!

Serves 6
Prep 5 mins
Cook 35 mins

5 apples
4 tbsp maple syrup or runny honey
2 tsp ground cinnamon
240g (3 cups) rolled oats
75g butter (I use vegan)
200g fresh raspberries

1. Preheat the oven to 200°C/180°C fan/gas 6.

2. Peel the apples and chop into equal-sized cubes.

3. Add to a pan over a low heat with 2 tablespoons maple syrup or honey, the cinnamon and 1 tablespoon water. Stir and simmer with the lid on for 10 minutes.

4. Meanwhile, make the oat crumble topping by adding 160g (2 cups) of oats to a blender and whizzing into a flour.

5. To a large bowl, add the oat flour, 80g (1 cup) rolled oats, the butter and remaining 2 tablespoons maple syrup and mix together with your hands.

6. Add the cooked apples to a large baking dish or 6 ramekins along with the berries and mix.

7. Finally, top with the crumble mixture and bake for 25 minutes until golden brown.

FAQ

Which apples do you use? Any will work so use what you have/prefer.

Can I use porridge oats? Yes, they will work too, it just adds less texture to the crumble topping.

Could I use frozen berries instead? Yes, follow the same instructions.

Do you have a cream recipe to top it with? Yes, try my Vanilla Cashew Cream on page 192.

BLUEBERRY GALETTES

How to make your very own gluten-free and vegan pastry in minutes! This galette is a great dinner party dessert that will really impress family and friends.

Makes 3
Prep 10 mins
Cook 15 mins
Cool 5–7 mins

250g plain flour (I use gluten-free), plus extra for dusting
125g salted butter (I use vegan)
50g coconut sugar
2 tbsp water
250g fresh or frozen blueberries
3 tsp maple syrup or runny honey

1. Preheat the oven to 220°C/200°C fan/gas 7.

2. To a bowl, add the flour, cubed butter and sugar and mix together with your hands until it forms a dough.

3. Now, add the water and mix together again until you form a large ball.

4. Flour your work surface and cut the dough into 3 pieces.

5. Gently roll out a piece of dough into a rough round shape, aiming for 5mm thick, and place onto a baking tray lined with baking paper.

6. Add a third of the blueberries into the middle and fold up the edges around the blueberries to enclose. Repeat with the remaining dough.

7. Finally, drizzle the sweetener of choice onto the blueberries and bake for 15 minutes.

8. Remove from the oven and allow to cool for 5–7 minutes, which helps the pastry to go crispy.

FAQ

Why is the pastry soft when baked? As the pastry isn't blind baked, which saves time, it has a slightly crispy outer layer but it's still soft on the inside.

Will this work with other berries? Absolutely, try it with blackberries or raspberries or you could even use a mixture.

How long will these last? They're best when eaten fresh, but you can make them earlier in the day and reheat or leave them overnight in a stored container at room temperature, though they will soften.

Can I use other sugar? Sure, swap the coconut sugar for brown sugar.

CHOCOLATE BROWNIES

The easiest brownies you'll ever make: 5 ingredients
and 5 minutes of prep.

Makes 9 squares
Prep 5 mins
Cook 15 mins
Cool 30–45 mins

300g self-raising flour
(I use gluten-free)
175g coconut sugar
75g cacao powder
60ml (¼ cup) oil
400ml milk of choice

1. Firstly, preheat the oven to 200°C/180°C fan/gas 6.

2. Add the flour, coconut sugar, cacao powder, oil and milk to
   a large bowl and whisk by hand until a smooth batter forms.

3. Line a 23cm (9 inch) square baking tray with baking paper,
   pour in the mix and smooth over the top.

4. Bake for 15 minutes.

5. Remove the brownie from the oven and allow to cool for
   30–45 minutes in the tin.

6. Slice into squares and they are ready to serve.

FAQ

Can I add a topping? Yes, spread over
my Easy Chocolate Ganache recipe on
page 198 when the brownie is cool.

Which oil did you use? Sunflower, but
other oils such as melted coconut will
work too.

How do I store them? Store in an airtight
container in the fridge for up to 2 days
(they will firm up the longer you leave
them in the fridge).

Can you swap for another sugar? Yes,
swap for granulated sugar if you wish.

PEANUT BUTTER BANANA BREAD

Love peanut butter? This banana bread made with peanut butter is the next level up for you to try. A great way of using up those ripe bananas.

Makes 8 large slices
Prep 10 mins
Cook 35 mins
Cool 10 mins

4 ripe bananas
1 tsp vanilla extract
2 tbsp peanut butter
80g coconut sugar
125ml (½ cup) milk of choice
3 tsp baking powder
250g plain flour
   (I use gluten-free)

1. Preheat the oven to 220°C/200°C fan/gas 7.

2. Peel and mash 3 of the ripe bananas in a large bowl.

3. Add the vanilla extract and peanut butter and mix together.

4. Now, add the sugar, milk, baking powder and flour and whisk by hand to a smooth batter.

5. Line a loaf tin with baking paper and pour in the batter.

6. Finally, slice the last banana down the middle lengthways and place on top.

7. Bake for 35 minutes in the middle of the oven.

8. Remove from the oven, slowly remove from the loaf tin and place onto a cooling rack for 10 minutes to cool before slicing.

FAQ

Peanut allergy? Swap for almond or cashew butter.

Nut allergy? Swap for seed butters instead or just leave the peanut butter out.

Does crunchy or smooth peanut butter matter? No, use what you have/love.

Which other sugar can I use? Brown sugar is a good swap for the coconut sugar.

What size loaf tin did you use? 900g (2lb).

DOUBLE-CHOCOLATE MUFFINS

I've yet to find gluten-free and vegan muffins as good as these.
And you can make them at home with ingredients you'll likely
have in the cupboard!

Serves 6
Prep 5 mins
Cook 20 mins
Cool 10–15 mins

250g self-raising flour
  (I use gluten-free)
150g coconut sugar
55g (½ cup) cacao powder
60ml (¼ cup) oil
300ml milk of choice
100g chocolate (I use vegan)

1. Preheat the oven to 200°C/180°C fan/gas 6.

2. To a large bowl, add the flour, sugar, cacao powder, oil and milk and whisk by hand into a smooth batter.

3. Roughly chop the chocolate into small chunks, add to the bowl and mix them through.

4. Line a cupcake tin with 6 liners and fill each one right to the top.

5. Bake for 20 minutes.

6. Remove the muffins from the cupcake tin onto a cooling rack and allow to cool for 10–15 minutes.

FAQ

Can I frost these? Yes, try my Easy Chocolate Ganache recipe on page 198 or Vanilla Cashew Cream on page 192. If using these, allow the muffins to cool before topping.

Can I use other sugar? Yes, swap the coconut sugar for brown sugar.

How long will they last? For 2 days in a sealed container at room temperature, but they're definitely best served on the day of baking.

Which oil did you use? Sunflower, but other oils such as melted coconut will work too.

NO-BAKE CHOCOLATE TART

One of the most popular desserts I have made to date, this chocolate tart is incredibly easy to make, decadent and uses just six ingredients.

Serves 10
Prep 10 mins
Chill 1–3 hours

1 tin (400ml) full-fat coconut milk
300g chocolate (I use vegan)
300g ground almonds
55g (½ cup) cacao powder
85ml (⅓ cup) maple syrup
3 tbsp melted coconut oil

1. Add the coconut milk to a pan and warm up over a low heat. Once warm, turn off the heat, break in the chocolate and stir until it melts and creates a sauce.

2. Now, make the base by adding the ground almonds, cacao powder, maple syrup and melted coconut oil to a large bowl and mixing until it starts to stick together.

3. Pour the base into a 23cm (9 inch) deep fluted tart tin and press down and around the sides until compact (you're looking for a roughly 3mm depth).

4. Pour the chocolate sauce over the base and place in the fridge for 3 hours or in the freezer for 1–2 hours until it has firmed up.

5. If you wish, decorate with fresh berries and my Vanilla Cashew Cream (page 192).

FAQ

Can you make this nut free? Absolutely, just swap the ground almonds for oat flour or desiccated coconut.

Can I use another oil? Sure, use sunflower oil.

How long will it last? This will keep in the fridge for up to 5 days if covered.

What chocolate works best? Try to go for a milkier chocolate as high % cacao ones are quite bitter. This tart doesn't have a lot of other sweetness added so the choice of chocolate is quite important.

UPSIDE-DOWN LEMON CAKE

Sharp and tangy with a hint of sweetness, a delicious cake that will totally impress family and friends.

Makes 8–10 slices
Prep 15 mins
Cook 35 mins
Cool 15 mins

2½ lemons
50g butter (I use vegan)
165g coconut sugar
250g plain flour
   (I use gluten-free)
1 tbsp baking powder
100g ground almonds
60ml (¼ cup) sunflower oil
200ml milk of choice

1. Firstly, preheat the oven to 200°C/180°C fan/gas 6.

2. Now, slice 1 of the lemons into thin circles, remove the pips and place into the bottom of a 20cm (8 inch) cake tin (preferably one with a removable bottom).

3. To a pan, add the butter, juice of ½ lemon and 40g of the coconut sugar. Place over a low heat and stir until a liquid forms.

4. Pour the liquid over the sliced lemon and place to one side.

5. To a large bowl, add the flour, baking powder, ground almonds, remaining sugar and zest and juice of 1 lemon. Pour in the oil and milk and mix to a smooth batter.

6. Spoon the batter over the lemons and bake for 30 minutes.

7. Remove from the oven and allow to cool slightly for 15 minutes.

8. Finally, get a large plate, unclip the sides of the cake tin, place the cake upside down onto the plate and remove the bottom of the cake tin to expose the lemons. The cake is now ready to slice.

FAQ

Can I make it nut free? Sure, just swap the ground almonds for extra flour.

What milk did you use? Almond.

Can I use other sugar? Yes, swap for golden caster sugar.

GOOEY NUT-BUTTER CHOC POT

The most popular blog recipe I have ever made. These are the ideal dessert when you need that chocolatey fix and are ready in under 15 minutes!

Serves 1
Prep 5 mins
Cook 10–12 mins

3 heaped tbsp rolled oats
3 tbsp cacao powder
½ tsp baking powder
tiny pinch of salt
1½ tbsp maple syrup or honey
60ml (¼ cup) milk of choice
1 tsp peanut or almond butter

1. Preheat the oven to 200°C/180°C fan/gas 6.

2. Create your oat flour by adding the oats to a blender for 30–60 seconds until they form a fine flour.

3. Now add the oat flour, cacao powder, baking powder and a tiny pinch of salt to a bowl and whisk by hand until there are no lumps.

4. Pour in the maple syrup or honey and milk and whisk into a smooth batter.

5. Add a spoonful of nut butter to a ramekin pot.

6. Pour the mixture into the ramekin and bake for 10 minutes.

7. Finally, allow to cool for a minute before eating. It should still be gooey in the middle and slightly firm on the top and sides.

FAQ

Nut allergy? Replace the nut butter with a square of chocolate or you could just leave the middle empty.

Can I use another flour? Sure, try plain flour instead.

Why wasn't mine gooey? You probably baked it too long, so next time reduce the cooking time by 1–2 minutes.

Can you microwave it instead? Yes, for roughly 90–120 seconds, but I think it tastes better when baked.

CONVERSION CHARTS

Conversions are approximate and have been rounded up or down.
Follow one set of measurements only – do not mix metric and imperial.

WEIGHT CONVERSIONS

METRIC	IMPERIAL
10g	¼oz
15g	½oz
20g	¾oz
25g/30g	1oz
35g	1¼oz
40g	1½oz
50g	1¾oz
55g	2oz
60g	2¼oz
70g	2½oz
75g/80g	2¾oz
85g	3oz
100g	3½oz
110g	3¾oz
115g	4oz
120g	4¼oz
125g	4½oz
140g	5oz
150g	5½oz
160g	5¾oz
170g/175g	6oz
180g	6¼oz
200g	7oz
225g	8oz
250g	9oz
280g/285g	10oz
300g	10½oz
320g	11¼oz
325g	11½oz
340g	11¾oz
350g	12oz
375g	13oz
390g	13½oz
400g	14oz
425g	15oz
450g	1lb
500g	1lb 2oz
600g	1lb 5oz
750g	1lb 10oz
900g	2lb
1kg	2lb 4oz
1.3kg	3lb
1.5kg	3lb 5oz
1.6kg	3lb 8oz
2kg	4lb 8oz
2.7kg	6lb

VOLUME CONVERSIONS (LIQUIDS)

METRIC	IMPERIAL	IMPERIAL/CUPS
5ml	1 teaspoon	
15ml	1 tablespoon	
30ml	1fl oz	2 tablespoons
45ml	3 tablespoons	
50ml	2fl oz	
60ml	4 tablespoons	¼ cup
75ml	2½fl oz	⅓ cup
90ml	6 tablespoons	
100ml	3½fl oz	
120ml/125ml	4fl oz	½ cup
150ml	5fl oz (¼ pint)	⅔ cup
185ml	6fl oz	¾ cup
200ml	7fl oz	
225ml	8fl oz	
250ml	9fl oz	1 cup
300ml	10fl oz (½ pint)	
350ml	12fl oz	1½ cups
400ml	14fl oz	
425ml	15fl oz (¾ pint)	
500ml	18fl oz	2 cups
600ml	20fl oz (1 pint)	
700ml	1¼ pints	
900ml	1½ pints	
1 litre	1¾ pints	4 cups
1.2 litres	2 pints	
1.7 litres	3 pints	

VOLUME CONVERSIONS (DRY INGREDIENTS – AN APPROXIMATE GUIDE)

Flour	125g	1 cup
Sugar	200g	1 cup
Butter	225g	1 cup (2 sticks)
Breadcrumbs (dried)	125g	1 cup
Nuts	125g	1 cup
Seeds	160g	1 cup
Dried fruit	150g	1 cup
Dried pulses (large)	175g	1 cup
Grains and small pulses	200g	1 cup

LENGTH

METRIC	IMPERIAL
5mm/½cm	¼ inch
1cm	½ inch
2cm	¾ inch
2.5cm	1 inch
3cm	1¼ inches
4cm	1½ inches
5cm	2 inches
5.5cm	2¼ inches
6cm	2½ inches
7cm	2¾ inches
7.5cm	3 inches
8cm	3¼ inches
9cm	3½ inches
10cm	4 inches
11cm	4¼ inches
12cm	4½ inches
13cm	5 inches
15cm	6 inches
18cm	7 inches
20cm	8 inches
23cm	9 inches
24cm	9½ inches
25cm	10 inches
26cm	10½ inches
27cm	10¾ inches
28cm	11 inches
30cm	12 inches
31cm	12½ inches
33cm	13 inches
34cm	13½ inches
35cm	14 inches
36cm	14¼ inches
38cm	15 inches
40cm	16 inches
41cm	16¼ inches
43cm	17 inches
44cm	17½ inches
46cm	18 inches

OVEN TEMPERATURES

°C	°C WITH FAN	°F	GAS MARK
110°C	90°C	225°F	¼
120°C	100°C	250°F	½
140°C	120°C	275°F	1
150°C	130°C	300°F	2
160°C	140°C	325°F	3
170°C	150°C	340°F	3½
180°C	160°C	350°F	4
190°C	170°C	375°F	5
200°C	180°C	400°F	6
220°C	200°C	425°F	7
230°C	210°C	450°F	8
240°C	220°C	475°F	9

CONVERSION CHARTS

INDEX

ACKNOWLEDGEMENTS

Firstly, I want to thank my wife Luise for the incredible support she has shown me throughout our time together and the passion she has shown towards my career path in food. Our story together shows what an amazing and caring person she is and without her support, I definitely wouldn't be in this position right now.

Secondly, my parents Sheila and Simon! They have supported everything I have done in my life, from my schoolwork, driving me everywhere to take part in sports and now the food blogging. My illness really scared them, not knowing if I was ever going to get better. I know they're incredibly proud of what I have achieved and without their support during the toughest times of my life you wouldn't be reading this book right now. They also allowed me to destroy their kitchen and helped wash up for over a week whilst I tested recipes in this book, so thank you for that!

My thanks also to:

My brand agent Leigh Rodda, who has helped and supported me enormously over the past few years and has really brought the best out of my content.

My book agent Caroline Wood for believing in me and helping me write my proposal that would land this book deal.

My amazing publisher Headline Home for giving me this incredible opportunity. It's something I've dreamt of doing since starting the blog 5 years ago and they made this all possible.

Lindsey Evans, publishing director at Headline Home, for really believing in me and allowing me the freedom I wanted when writing this cookbook. And many thanks to everyone else at Headline who has helped me along the way, including Kathryn Allen, Siobhan Hooper, Kate Miles, Jessica Farrugia and Fergus Edmondson.

Kay Halsey, for spending hours and hours helping with the editing and layout of this book.

Clare Skeats, who designed this book and made it flow so beautifully.

The three who really helped make the food look amazing in this book!

Clare Winfield, who shot all the amazing recipes and was such a lovely person to work with.

Emma Lahaye, who styled all the recipes so beautifully. Her vision and expertise really helped bring the food to life and made it the key focus.

Jess Geddes, who spent 10 days cooking my recipes for the photoshoot. She worked incredibly hard and helped so much.

And finally, I want to say a big thank you to YOU! For following my journey, believing in me and for buying my cookbook. Without the support I have received over the years since starting my blog this book wouldn't have been possible. Thank you!

Copyright © 2022 James Wythe
The right of James Wythe to be identified as the author of
the work has been asserted by him in accordance with the
Copyright, Designs and Patents Act 1988.

Photography © Clare Winfield 2021

First published in 2022
by Headline Home
An imprint of Headline Publishing Group

1

Apart from any use permitted under UK copyright law, this publication may only
be reproduced, stored, or transmitted, in any form, or by any means, with prior permission
in writing of the publishers or, in the case of reprographic production, in accordance
with the terms of licences issued by the Copyright Licensing Agency.

Every effort has been made to fulfil requirements with regard to reproducing
copyright material. The author and publisher will be glad to rectify any omissions
at the earliest opportunity.

Cataloguing in Publication Data is available from the British Library

ISBN 978 1 4722 8958 2

eISBN 978 1 4722 8959 9

Commissioning Editor: Lindsey Evans
Designed by Clare Skeats
Photography: Clare Winfield
Food and prop styling: Emma Lahaye
Food styling assistant: Jess Geddes
Project editors: Kay Halsey and Kate Miles
Assistant editor: Kathryn Allen
Proofreaders: Vicky Orchard and Amber Burlinson
Indexer: Caroline Wilding
Photography (wedding photo) page 12 © Tom and Lizzie Redman
Photography page 15 © Laura Bailey
Photography page 22 © James Wythe

MIX
Paper from
responsible sources
FSC® C011124

Headline's policy is to use papers that are natural, renewable and recyclable
products and made from wood grown in sustainable forests. The logging and
manufacturing processes are expected to conform to the environmental
regulations of the country of origin.

Printed and bound in Germany by Mohn Media

Colour reproduction by Alta London Ltd.

HEADLINE PUBLISHING GROUP
An Hachette UK Company
Carmelite House
50 Victoria Embankment
London EC4Y 0DZ

www.headline.co.uk
www.hachette.co.uk